P9-DHF-317

A Patchwork Alphabet

by Eileen Westfall

Meredith® Press
New York

Acknowledgments

Thank you to the following special people who helped me with the preparation of this book.

Shel Izen, for the photographs.

Darrel Young, for the graphic artwork.

Katherine Bilton, who made the samples for the Fifty-Four-Forty or Fight Wallhanging and the Windblown Square Quilt, and for her quilting on the Patchwork Alphabet Quilt.

Marta Estes, who did the quilting on the Kansas Trouble and Prairie Queen quilts.

Colleen Gidner, who designed and made the teddy bears used as props for the Round the Corner and Union Square projects.

Shirley Gundlach, who made the samples for the Independence Square Table Runner and Napkin Rings.

Carol Hart, for framing mats used for individual quilt blocks.

Cathie Helgeland, for all dried flower arrangements.

Carol Porter, who made the sample for the Heart and Home Wallhanging.

Nadene Stephenson, for antique quilts used as props.

Nancy Sweeney, who made the sample for the Grape Basket Quilt and the top for the Prairie Queen Quilt.

Jana Baldridge Vargas, who made the samples for the Jacob's Ladder Apron and Potholder, Temperance Tree Pillows, Union Square Mini Quilt and Wallhanging, Young Man's Fancy Tablecloth and Chair Back, and blocks "H" through "Z" of the Patchwork Alphabet Quilt.

Sue von Jentzen, who made the Bear Paw Quilt, Ohio Star blocks, the Quilter's Surprise Wallhanging, and the Variable Star and Magnolia Bud Wallhanging top.

The Monroe Historical Society, for the use of the Shannahan Cabin (c. 1887), the first building of Monroe, Washington.

ISBN: 0-696-02388-1
First Printing: 1993
Library of Congress Card Catalog Number: 92-085377
Published by Meredith® Press
Distributed by Meredith® Corporation, Des Moines, Iowa

10 9 8 7 6 5 4 3 2 1

All rights reserved.

Printed in the United States of America

Copyright © 1993 Eileen Westfall. All rights reserved. No part of this book may be reproduced or used in any form without permission in writing from Meredith® Corporation.

Meredith® Press is an imprint of Meredith® Books
President, Book Group: Joseph J. Ward
Vice-President, Editorial Director: Elizabeth P. Rice

For Meredith Press:
Executive Editor: Maryanne Bannon
Associate Editor: Ruth A. Weadock
Production Manager: Bill Rose
Design: Diane Wagner
Cover design: Remo Cosentino, BookGraphics

Packaged by Rapid Transcript,
a division of March Tenth, Inc.
Project Editor: Cyndi Marsico

With loving memory to my father,
Hilman Kurth.
He believed in me and bought me
my first sewing machine.

Dear Crafter,

Some quilters are renowned for their technical expertise; others for their design; others for their diversity. Eileen Westfall, the author of *A Patchwork Alphabet,* is the quintessential quilting artist, using the selection and coordination of fabrics coupled with meticulous design to express the inherent variety and beauty of her craft.

A Patchwork Alphabet is more than just a collection of 27 delightful, country–inspired projects—each chapter includes the actual-size templates for a full-size quilt block, providing the patterns and directions that will enable you to express your own quilting visions in any number of personally designed projects.

The gorgeous, full-color illustrations of each finished project and Eileen's friendly, inviting tone throughout the helpful "Basics" chapter and project introductions, plus clear, easy-to-follow directions, add further to the pleasure of working with this book.

We at Meredith® Press take every measure to ensure that our crafting books are of the highest quality for our readers. We are proud to offer *A Patchwork Alphabet,* and we send you our warmest wishes for success in all your quilting endeavors.

Sincerely,

MARYANNE BANNON
Executive Editor

Contents

◆◆◆◆◆◆◆◆◆◆

Introduction

◆◆◆◆◆◆◆◆◆◆

When I came up with the concept for the *Patchwork Alphabet*, it had been a while since my last book was published, and I had been tossing around ideas for my next one for some time.

My creativity is nourished by surrounding myself with beautiful and creative things, so I went to see an exhibit called "Son of Heaven," a display of treasures once owned by several emperors of China, which was in its final days at the Seattle Center. The show was incredible—room after room filled with fabulous sculpture, jewelry, tapestries, and furniture—some of the most exquisite items I had ever seen.

While driving home afterward, my creative juices bubbling from the sheer beauty and craftsmanship of the exhibit, the idea of a patchwork alphabet came to me.

Later that same evening I began designing the first project, the Patchwork Alphabet Quilt. Then I began looking up patterns, one for each letter of the alphabet, in my many patchwork encyclopedias. Within a few days, I had enough material to provide the basis of a book proposal.

The next step was designing the rest of the projects, the inspiration for which came from various sources, such as books, magazines, movies, and the beauty of nature. I sketched my designs on graph paper with a pencil, then I redrew them with a pen and filled them in with colored pencils.

Next, I decided which samples I would make and which I would have made by other people. I belong to a quilting group called Ladies of the Block, which is part of a guild called Quilters Anonymous. All the members of my group are expert quilters, and I hired them to make the project samples that I chose not to make myself.

Because I feel that the fabric used in a project is just as important an element as the design itself, I did all of the fabric selection for the samples myself, regardless of who was to actually make them. Some of the samples were made from my own supply of fabric, and some are the results of purchases at fabric shops.

One of the most enjoyable aspects of preparing this book was being in charge of the photography. One of the least enjoyable aspects was finding a photographer. I didn't know any professional ones, so I called a few whose listings I saw in the telephone book, but none of them seemed right for *A Patchwork Alphabet.*

Finally, a friend recommended Shel Izen, a photographer with whom she herself had worked, and I made an appointment to meet with him at his studio in the charming Wedgewood area of Seattle. I felt right at home in his studio, which had a creative atmosphere and was decorated with forest green (one of my favorite colors) and warm woods, and after talking with him, I was sure that he was the perfect photographer for my book.

All of the photographs in *A Patchwork Alphabet* (except the cover shot) were taken in my family room, bedroom, and other living areas of my house in Edmonds, Washington. Shel would arrive at our early morning sessions with bagels and cream cheese, and I would have classical music playing, for inspiration. Our sessions were often hectic and sometimes lasted up to twelve hours each, but we were always in creative agreement and worked with shared enthusiasm, and I couldn't be happier with the results.

My home is one of the historic houses in town. Built in 1904, it was originally the sanctuary for the Edmonds Methodist Church and was located on the main street. After a while, a larger sanctuary was built and the former church became the pastor's home. When the pastor moved out, the house was used as the fellowship hall. In the 1930s, the church burned to the ground, leaving only the house standing, which the congregation sold after deciding to start over in a different location. The new owners had the house moved up the street onto the lot where I now live.

When I bought the house in 1982, it was a real fixer-upper, whose main selling point was its gorgeous view of Puget Sound. Since then, creative vision and lots of work have helped restore the house to its former beauty, which I am happy to share with you in the pages of this book.

I hope you like the projects in *A Patchwork Alphabet* as much as I enjoyed designing them for you. And I trust that you will feel challenged and gratified as you make them.

Yours warmly,

Eileen Westfall

EILEEN WESTFALL

1 All About Patchwork

Basic Equipment

There's an old saying: "It's a poor workman who blames his tools." However, in quiltmaking it is essential that you use the proper equipment. When you do, any quilting project will proceed more easily and accurately, and the possibility of needless frustration will have been reduced.

This section discusses basic tools and materials needed in order to achieve the best results possible when making the projects in *A Patchwork Alphabet*.

Glue Sticks

Because they have a waxy base, glue sticks are neat, clean, and easy to use, which makes them ideal for holding fabric shapes in place for appliqué. Be sure the glue stick you use is suitable for use on fabric.

Light Boxes

A light box is a handy piece of equipment for marking quilting, embroidery, and other designs on fabric. It is used as a light source behind the pattern and the piece of fabric to be marked, so that the design lines will show through clearly to the front of the fabric. (See "The Quilt Layers" on page 14 for other methods of backlighting.)

Light boxes are low, rectangular frames that come in a wide range of sizes—some as small as 12″ × 10″—with a smooth, translucent top surface and one or more bulbs or tubes inside for providing illumination.

Used mostly by graphic artists and photographers, light boxes can be purchased in art-supply stores.

Marking Pencils—No!

I have a collection of antique quilts. A few of them show the remnants of the marking methods of yesteryear—done with a regular pencil—which ruin the look of my quilts. In the days when those quilts were made, quilters did not yet have the advantage of the erasable marking tools that we have now.

I do *not* recommend using the temporary marking pencils that are on the market today, because the ones I have seen do not come with adequate removal instructions.

A woman who quilted a sample for one of my books used a yellow marking pencil on it. She called me in a panic and said that she had completed the quilting but could not get the pencil marks out. I worked on the piece myself, scrubbing it with a prewash stain-removal stick—and risking the possibility of fading the fabric colors! After many hours of scrubbing and soaking, the pencil marks faded enough for the photograph of the sample to be shot, but the piece still has visible yellow marks on it to this day.

Marking Pens—Yes!

Erasable marking pens are available with two different kinds of ink: the kind that fades over time and the kind that washes out with water. Each type has advantages and disadvantages.

The fading-ink type of pen makes light markings, which may fade before a project is completed, creating the need to mark the piece again. (I use fading-ink markers only on small projects that I know will be completed quickly.)

The other type of ink, which washes out with water, is usually a bright color. Traces may reappear after drying. It may have to be rewet many times before the markings disappear entirely.

Needles and Pins

Quilting needles are called "betweens" and are so marked on their packages, which usually contain an assortment of needles in sizes #7 through #12. The higher the number, the finer the needle, with #12 needles being the finest. The smaller the needle, the easier it is to make the tiny, neat stitches required for hand-quilting and sewing.

Be sure to use the best pins available, even if they seem expensive. Dull pins can snag and pull fabric, and they are hard to work with. Silk pins or ball-tip pins are the sharpest and therefore, glide through fabric most smoothly. Quilter's pins are longer than regular pins and have round, colored heads that are more easily seen than flat-headed pins for removal from fabric. As someone who has been stuck by many stray pins, I highly recommend quilter's pins for their ease of use as well as for their visibility.

Quilting Hoops and Frames

Quilting hoops are similar to embroidery hoops, but they are sturdier because they have to stabilize several thicknesses of fabric during the quilting process. Some quilting hoops come with a stand attached.

A quilting frame is rectangular in shape and usually large enough to accommodate a full-size quilt, which is pinned to the frame and then stabilized along the sides every few inches. An entire group of quilters can work together around a frame set up in a large room such as a basement, and the frame was a staple for quilters of the past.

Most quilters today find frames too large and cumbersome to have in their homes and prefer using hoops instead.

Quilting Tape

Quilting tape is a paper tape (also known as masking tape) that is available in hardware stores as well as in quilting shops. It comes in various widths—some as narrow as 1/64"—and can help your quilting have a more professional look.

The tape is applied directly onto the item being quilted, as a stitching guide for the quilter to follow, so that lines of stitching will be perfectly straight. Quilting tape is relatively inflexible, so it is generally not suitable for use on curves.

Rotary Cutters

Rotary cutters have revolutionized patchwork. They are the most accurate tool available for cutting straight edges. I highly recommend using a rotary cutter, but I also recommend becoming proficient in its use before attempting to cut your patchwork pieces: Without practice, you could cut yourself or ruin your fabric. If needed, stop into your fabric or quilt shop and ask for assistance in learning how to use a rotary cutter.

Be sure to use a special self-sealing mat under anything you cut with a rotary cutter to avoid marring your work surface. Self-sealing mats are made of a resistant plastic that enables even deep cuts to appear to heal themselves, leaving only surface scratches visible. Most cutting mats have ruler markings along the outer edges and a grid in the center for easy measuring and accurate cutting.

Scissors

It is important to keep a separate pair of scissors for cutting fabric only. Have several other pairs on hand for cutting paper and other materials.

Be sure all of your scissors are sharp, so that cutting will go as smoothly as possible. If any of your scissors have become dull, sharpen them.

Seam Rippers

In a craft as exacting as patchwork, mistakes are bound to happen. If you make a mistake, don't get discouraged. So long as you correct your errors neatly, no harm will have been done.

If a seam needs to be taken out and restitched, using a seam ripper can sure beat the time and painstaking effort required to remove the stitches with a pin.

Sewing Machines

Every project in this book requires the use of a sewing machine. Make sure yours is in good working order and has been oiled recently before you begin. Start each project with a new needle, using a size appropriate for sewing cotton fabric.

I own an inexpensive, basic, no-frills sewing machine that makes straight and zigzag stitches. It isn't computerized, and it doesn't do a multitude of decorative stitches, but it's a great sewing machine and does all I need for any quilting project.

Thimbles

I have a confession to make: In the many years that I have been sewing, I have never been able to feel comfortable using a thimble. (I am left-handed, and I do many things upside-down or backwards, which could be the source of what I call my "thimble block.")

I have tried every kind of thimble made—even the soft leather ones—but I have never found one that I was really comfortable with. So I work without a thimble, and my fingers bleed whenever I work on a large quilting project.

I don't recommend quilting without a thimble. Do yourself a favor and use one. A thimble will protect your fingers and push the needle more easily through the fabric—and you will be able to enjoy painless quilting.

Thread

In my early days of sewing, I made a yellow patchwork item and used navy blue thread to stitch it together. I didn't have any yellow thread on hand at the time, and I wasn't aware that it would be a mistake to use a contrasting color thread. The navy blue that I used showed through and gave the item an overall dingy look. I learned an important lesson from that project: Always use sewing thread that matches the fabric!

Another important factor is the type of thread you use. When sewing cotton patchwork or appliqué projects, use only 100-percent cotton thread. Polyester thread will pull and pucker.

For quilting, use only special quilting thread, which is pretreated with wax and is made coarser than regular sewing thread, so that it will be strong enough to withstand the strain of being pulled through three layers of material for quilting. The coarseness also lends strength to the quilt, adding to its overall durability. Many of the antique quilts in my collection have fabric that is faded and torn, but their quilting stitches are still intact.

Quilting thread comes in all colors. Many interesting effects can be achieved with the use of a contrasting color, so don't be afraid to experiment. I prefer quilting with white or cream-colored thread, but color choice is solely a matter of individual taste.

Fabric

I have several friends whose greatest joy in life seems to be finding fabric in unusual places—just for the sake of accumulating more. They stop at every garage sale, they pick through thrift shops, and they love to talk about their latest acquisitions. For some of them, collecting fabric has become an addiction.

I never purchase fabric just for the sake of accumulating more. I only buy fabric that I know I will use.

Choosing fabric is a subjective matter—what is beautiful to one person is not necessarily beautiful to another. In this section I share with you my outlook on fiber content and color as they relate to patchwork, as well as offer some guidelines for fabric selection, combination, preparation, and storage.

Fiber Content

Use only 100-percent cotton fabric when making patchwork projects. Polyester and polyester blends pucker and pull, and they don't give the fine results that all-cotton fabric does.

Here are two methods of testing whether your fabric is 100-percent cotton.

The flame test. Pull a few threads from the fabric and hold them (carefully!) over a flame. Polyester and other synthetics will give off black smoke and have the faint smell of plastic.

The ironing test. Iron the fabric. All-cotton fabric will crease more easily than will polyester or other synthetics.

Color

Everyone has favorite colors—colors that they tend to gravitate toward. Color is as important an aspect of patchwork as design is. It plays a large part in whether or not an item is aesthetically pleasing.

I recently consulted a color professional, who did an analysis by draping me with an assortment of fabric swatches in both cool and warm colors. (Warm colors are those that have predominant undertones of red or yellow; cool colors are those that have undertones of blue.)

I was told that my skin tones are most compatible with warm colors and that I'm a "spring." (Color analysts break down color types into seasons.) Springs, I was told, are in the minority of color types, which didn't surprise me, because I've always been attracted to different colors than most of my friends have. I learned that the colors I choose to live with and to create quilts in—greens, peaches, and purples—are warm colors. (My quilting group thinks I am kind of strange for being the only member whose favorite color isn't blue and who doesn't have a house filled with blues.)

Some information and tips follow to help you choose pleasing colors for your projects, whatever your personal preferences are.

Colors, tones, tints, and shades. There are three **primary colors,** the colors from which all others are derived: yellow, red, and blue (indicated in boldface on the Color Wheel). The **secondary colors** (those halfway between the primary colors on the wheel) are orange, violet—or purple—and green. The **tertiary colors** (those between the primary and secondary colors on the wheel) are yellow-orange, red-orange, red-violet, blue-violet, blue-green, and yellow-green.

White, black, gray, and beige (which don't appear on the wheel) are considered **neutral tones** and not colors.

A **tint** is created when white is added to a color.

A **shade** is created when black is added to a color.

Color schemes. There are three main types of color schemes: monochromatic, analogous, and complementary.

A **monochromatic** scheme combines shades or tints of the same color.

An **analogous** scheme combines related colors, those that are next to each other on the Color Wheel.

A **complementary** scheme combines colors that are opposite each other on the wheel.

Color values. I prefer a formula of dark-value colors for the dominant pieces in my blocks, medium-value colors for the secondary pieces, and light-value colors or neutral tones for the background pieces. This formula can also be effective in reverse: light-value colors or neutral tones for dominant pieces, medium-value colors for secondary pieces, and dark-value colors for background pieces. (Amish quilts often use this reverse color-value scheme.)

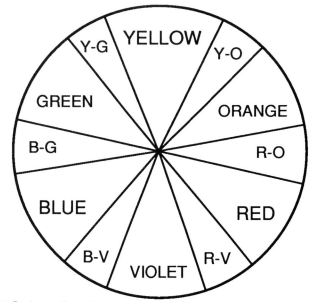

Fabric Selection

When I enter a fabric store, I go directly to the 100-percent cotton section. I look up and down the aisles, scanning the fabrics, and then I began narrowing my focus to specific colors and prints.

In order for me to want to buy a particular fabric, I have to feel excited about it—I have to hear a little voice inside me that says, "This is beautiful!" Although I might not have a specific project in mind for the fabric when I purchase it, the excitement I feel when I see it assures me that eventually it will look terrific in *something* and that it won't be given away or wind up collecting dust on a shelf.

What makes a fabric beautiful to me? If I have a strong, positive reaction to it, I just know it's what I want. (And if I have a similarly overpowering negative reaction to it, I just know it isn't for me.) However, not all fabric is that easily evaluated. When I come across fabric that I feel unsure about, I ask myself the following questions.

Do I really like the color? Have you ever seen a fabric print that you liked but wished it was available in a different color? A friend once showed me a great print that she had bought in a color we both knew she would never be able to live with. She loved the print, but disliking the color would prevent her from ever using that piece of fabric. She was out the money she had spent for it, plus she had to live with the disappointment of what might have been.

Even if you are crazy about a particular print, don't buy the fabric unless you're also crazy about the color.

If I like the color, do I also like the print? I enjoy using flowers, butterflies, or any motif that is realistic and easily recognizable; I don't like to use abstract prints.

I love small, delicate prints—flowers, buds, vines, and ferns. To me, smaller prints more closely resemble the fabrics used on the prairie by our quiltmaking ancestors, and that's the feel I like my prints to have. With their delicate lines and soft colors, they are such classics that they are beautiful even today.

There have been occasional trends over the years to use large, splashy prints in patchwork, and while I think that many of them are attractive, I also feel that they are too "busy" to work well in most patchwork. If you want to use large prints, use them only in large patchwork patterns.

Is the color compatible with other fabrics I want to use? When planning a project I usually pick the main fabric first and then the supporting ones. I take a swatch of the main fabric with me to the store, so that I can make sure the colors and prints are all compatible.

Unless the supporting fabrics seem as right as the main one, any project could be less than its best.

Fabric Combinations

When I'm not sure whether a particular fabric combination will work in a patchwork block, I test it before cutting out all of the fabric pieces for my project.

First, I make an actual-size drawing of the block on graph paper. Next, I determine which are the dominant design pieces, which are the secondary pieces, and which are the background pieces. Then I label my graph-paper shapes with "D," "S," and "B" accordingly.

After I have chosen fabrics that I think might work, I cut out just enough shapes from fabric (minus the seam allowance) to make one block, and I glue the shapes to my graph-paper pattern, creating an actual-size sample of my proposed block.

Using this method, you can try many different color and print combinations, thus avoiding the disappointment of discovering only after you've already cut out and stitched together all of the pieces that you don't have a pleasing combination.

Don't be afraid to experiment. Have fun with your fabrics. The possibilities are limited only by your imagination.

Fabric Preparation

Prewash all fabrics before beginning a project. If there is to be any fabric shrinkage, it should be eliminated before cutting and stitching and not after the project is completed.

To remind myself which of my fabrics were prewashed, I label one corner of each prewashed piece with a bright sticker.

Fabric Storage

It's useful to keep your fabric all together, so that you can see at a glance what you have. I store mine on shelves in a doorless closet. If you don't have a spare closet that you can devote to fabric, you could use a bookcase with deep shelves.

I stack my fabric, neatly folded, according to color. (I place complementary colors next to each other, for the sake of aesthetics.) When I'm looking for a print in a particular color, I take out the stack of that color and then look for the appropriate print.

It's also helpful to keep track of how much you have of each fabric. I keep a tag on my large fabric pieces with their yardage. Every time I use some fabric, I adjust the amount on its tag, so that I won't have to stop and measure how much I have the next time I'm considering using that fabric.

During the course of a project, my fabrics can get pretty disorganized. When I take the time to reorganize my fabric before starting each new project, I have a more together, orderly feel.

Patchwork

Patchwork is the piecing and stitching together of fabric shapes, to form a specific pattern. The following are some basic tips for successful patchwork.

Cutting Accurate Pieces

Accuracy is of the utmost importance in patchwork, and cutting fabric shapes is at the heart of that accuracy. It requires special care in preparing the fabric, in the marking of the templates on the fabric, and in the actual cutting.

Ironing. Before cutting out shapes, press the fabric with a hot steam iron. Wrinkles or folds in the fabric will prevent the shapes from being exact.

Placement on fabric. Cut shapes so that their straight edges are on the lengthwise and crosswise grain of the fabric, unless specifically directed otherwise. Pieces cut on the bias (the diagonal) of the fabric will have extra elasticity and may not fit the edges of the other patchwork pieces smoothly and accurately.

Marking shapes on fabric. On the wrong side of the fabric, either trace around the template with a marking pen (see "Basic Equipment," page 7), or pin the template in place.

Gluing a piece of sandpaper to the back of a paper template or shaped pattern, with the gritty side facing down, is a great trick for cutting out accurate shapes from fabric. The sandpaper adds weight and sturdiness to the paper shape, and the rough surface of the gritty side helps grip the fabric for a more accurate cut. Be sure to cut sandpaper only with old, dull shears, so that you won't ruin your good scissors.

Regardless of the type of paper from which your template is cut, be sure the pins that hold it against the fabric are placed closely together and as near the edges of the template as possible. If the template is bowed or wrinkled, the shape of the fabric piece will be distorted.

There is another "marking" method that some people use but which I strongly advise against: the hold-and-cut technique. Patchwork is an exact art, and holding a template against the fabric with one hand while cutting out the shape with the other hand is a method that can lead only to ill-shaped, ill-fitting fabric pieces and frustration.

Cutting the shapes. Use sharp scissors or a rotary cutter (see "Basic Equipment," page 8) to cut out accurate fabric shapes. Rotary cutters work best for cutting straight edges, but for cutting curves, use scissors.

Sewing Pieces Together

Perfectly cut fabric shapes alone will not make a successful project—they must be sewn together with precise care and accuracy.

Pin or baste the fabric. To prevent slipping before and during stitching, pin the seams to be joined, or baste them with contrasting thread. (Using contrasting thread will make removal of basting stitches easier.)

Use short stitches. Set the sewing machine for short, straight stitches, about 12 stitches-per-inch. Long, loose stitches can come undone, and small stitches will add to the overall strength of the patchwork.

Back-tack the seams. Stitch back and forth a short distance at both ends of each seam, to prevent it from coming undone.

Maintain uniform seam allowances. Most patchwork projects use ¼" seam allowances. Any variation from the specified seam allowance will cause the patchwork to be ill-fitted; that is, the seams will not meet as they should and the shape of the project will be distorted.

If your sewing machine doesn't have a stitching guide, you can use a piece of tape, placed exactly ¼" from the needle, to act as a guide.

Press the seam allowances. Iron all seam allowances toward the darker fabrics after stitching together individual pieces, strips, or blocks. Pressing the seam allowances in this manner will prevent darker seam allowances from showing through under lighter fabrics on the front of the project.

Lighter colors are usually the background of a patchwork block and are the most likely areas to be embroidered or quilted. Pressing seam allowances away from lighter pieces will also, therefore, eliminate unnecessary bulk through which you might otherwise have to push your embroidery or quilting needle.

Appliqué

Appliqué is the stitching of one fabric shape on another, larger one.

Quilts can be made in appliqué only—on a large, single piece of background fabric (such as Baltimore Album or Hawaiian quilts)—with no patchwork at all. They can also have appliqué done on individual, solid squares or blocks, creating a quilt that combines both patchwork and appliqué techniques.

Appliqué can be done with a sewing machine (which gives an item a modern look) or by hand (which gives a more traditional look). All the projects in this book that feature appliqué have been sewn by hand, but it is also possible to appliqué them by machine. The choice is yours.

Tips and directions for both types of appliqué follow.

Machine Appliqué

I used to do appliqué by machine exclusively, because it was quick and easy, and hand-appliqué seemed tedious. The main advantage of machine-appliqué is its speed.

One disadvantage is that unless you use a sewing machine that does great zigzag stitching, machine-appliqué can be frustrating. Machines can sometimes balk when making close-set zigzag stitches (satin stitch), which could result in the formation of a big knot of thread or tears in the fabric.

Another disadvantage is that machine-appliquéd edges can fray more easily in the washing machine than hand-appliquéd edges, and those edges can be difficult to repair.

Step 1: Cut out the fabric shape to be appliquéd; cut on the stitching line and do not add seam allowance.

Step 2: Using a glue stick, attach the fabric shape to the right side (front) of the background fabric, being careful to place it in the exact spot desired. Press it with a warm iron to secure.

Step 3: Cut out a piece of tear-away nonwoven interfacing that is slightly larger than the shape to be appliquéd.

Step 4: Pin the interfacing to the wrong side of the background fabric, so that it extends beyond the edges of the shape to be appliquéd. (The interfacing will add stability to the fabric during stitching.)

Step 5: Set the sewing machine for close-set zigzag stitches, about $\frac{1}{16}$" wide. Test the flow of stitching and the tension of the machine on a piece of scrap fabric; if bunching occurs, loosen the tension or reset the machine for stitches spaced a little further apart.

Step 6: Zigzag-stitch all around the edges of the shape being appliquéd, completely covering the edges with satin stitch, to prevent future fraying.

Step 7: After the fabric shape has been appliquéd, tear away the interfacing from the wrong side of the backing fabric.

Hand-Appliqué

After years of quilting, I have come to favor the look of hand-appliquéd items to that of machine-appliquéd ones. Even though appliqué takes more time by hand, it is a traditional method that produces a classic look which, to me, is well worth the extra time and effort.

There are many different methods of hand-appliqué, and stitching by hand can be a pleasure instead of a chore. My preferred method of hand-appliqué uses a paper template.

Step 1: Cut out the fabric shape to be appliquéd, including seam allowance.

Step 2: Trim away the seam allowance from the template (or make a second copy of the template, to avoid cutting the first one).

Step 3: Center the template that has no seam allowance on the wrong side of the fabric shape, and fold the seam allowance of the fabric smoothly over the edges to the back of the paper.

Step 4: Baste completely around the fabric shape.

Step 5: Press the fabric shape with a hot steam iron, to flatten the seam allowance and crease the folded edges.

Step 6: Remove the basting thread and the paper template from the fabric shape.

Step 7: Using a glue stick, attach the fabric shape to the right side (front) of the background fabric, being careful to place it in the exact spot desired. Press it with a warm iron to secure.

Step 8: Sew the fabric shape to the background fabric, making tiny overcast stitches. (Take stitches from underneath the fabric shape, instead of next to it, to hide them as well as possible.)

The Quilt Layers

Marking the Quilt Front

Adequate backlighting, an erasable marking pen, and a steady hand are the essentials for transferring quilting motifs, embroidery patterns, and other designs to the quilt front.

The desired pattern is placed between the light source and the fabric to be marked, so that the design lines show through to the front of the fabric for marking.

For backlighting, you can use a light box (see "Basic Equipment," page 7) or either of the two methods that follow.

The window method. For marking small items, you will need tape and a clean window that has lots of sunlight shining through it.

Step 1: Tape the pattern to the window.

Step 2: Tape the fabric piece to be marked over the pattern, so that the design is directly behind the spot where the marking is to be done.

Step 3: Trace the design onto the fabric.

The lamp method. For marking large items, you will need tape, a lamp with a shade that has a large circular top opening, and a clean pane of clear glass (such as from a picture frame) that is large enough to sit comfortably on top of the lampshade.

Step 1: Place the pane of glass securely on top of the lampshade.

Step 2: Tape the pattern to the glass and turn on the light.

Step 3: Place the fabric to be marked over the pattern, so that the design is directly under the spot where the marking is to be done.

Step 4: Trace the design onto the fabric, adjusting the pattern and fabric as necessary to mark the entire design.

The Batting

Batting is available in both prepackaged and on a roll (similar to fabric yard goods). In prepackaged form, batting is sold as a single, large piece that has been folded, rolled up, and then packaged. Prepackaged batting comes in standard sizes for crib-, twin-, full-, queen-, and king-size quilts.

On the roll, batting is usually 60″ wide and can be cut to whatever length you want. Batting by the yard can be less expensive than the prepackaged kind, but it may have to be pieced together to create a width large enough for your quilt.

Batting comes in various weights. I don't like to struggle through heavy batting when I'm quilting (my stitching seems to go much faster and much more enjoyably when I use lightweight batting), and I recommend using the lightest weight available.

If you decide to purchase batting by the yard and it isn't wide enough for your quilt, use the following method to piece it together to achieve the necessary width.

Step 1: Cut two pieces of batting to the length needed.

Step 2: Set the lengths side by side, with their inner edges touching but not overlapping, on a clean, flat surface, such as a floor or large table.

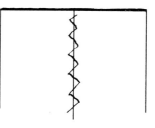

Step 3: Hand-sew the lengths of batting together, making wide zigzag stitches.

Step 4: Set the quilt front on top of the pieced batting, and trim the batting to the same size as the fabric.

Step 5: Remove the quilt front.

The Backing

I have seen many creative quilt backings. Some are every bit as decorative and attractive as the quilt front, and this type of quilt is called double-sided. I have also seen quilts with just a few blocks sewn to the backing. You can use your imagination and creativity to embellish your quilt backings any way you desire.

Because many fabrics are only 45″ wide, a backing wider than 45″ has to be pieced. A simple method of piecing the quilt backing follows.

Step 1: Cut two pieces of backing fabric to the length needed.

Step 2: Trim off one selvage edge from each fabric piece.

Step 3: Place the fabric pieces together, right sides in, matching up the cut selvage edges; pin or baste.

Step 4: Machine-stitch the cut selvage edges together with a ¼″ seam.

Step 5: Unfold the fabric and press the seam open, to prevent bulk in the center of the backing.

Step 6: Place the backing on a smooth, flat surface (I use the floor), wrong side up.

Step 7: Place the quilt front on top, centering it on the backing.

Step 8: Trim the backing, leaving 2″ extending beyond the edges of the quilt front at the top, bottom, and sides. (The extra fabric allows for shrinkage during the quilting process.)

Step 9: Remove the quilt front.

Setting the Quilt Together

To assemble the quilt layers, first place the backing, wrong side up, on a large, flat surface. Place the batting on top of the backing, centering it and leaving equal margins all around. Finally, set the quilt front, right side up, on the batting, matching edges.

Quilting

Quilting is a three-step process: First the quilt layers are basted together, then the actual quilting is done, and finally the basting is removed and the quilting designs pop out. These steps, quilting tips, and five different styles of quilting are discussed in this section.

Basting the Quilt

Basting together the quilt front, batting, and backing helps to stabilize the layers of the quilt and prevents bunching during the actual quilting. Basting is my least favorite part of the quiltmaking process, but it is an important step nonetheless. Without basting, a quilt front that has been carefully and painstakingly made can become hopelessly bunched, thus ruining the entire quilt.

I once made a wallhanging (one that I don't like to think about) that now lies buried deep in an old trunk. The front has a basket design that I worked on long and hard. I was in a hurry to begin quilting it as soon as the front was completed, and I did a sloppy and inadequate job of basting.

As I quilted it, I began to see puckers and small twists forming. I told myself that once the quilting was completed, my wallhanging would look okay. But the longer I quilted, the more I realized that I was paying the price for having cheated on the basting.

After quilting a few blocks and working some of the feather-stitch designs on the border, I sadly packed away the wallhanging, consoling myself with the prospect of someday tearing out all of the quilting, doing the basting properly, and then starting the quilting all over again. So far, I still haven't gotten around to it, and instead of being displayed on a wall for me to enjoy, my wallhanging lies hidden away.

The lesson I learned from my experience is this: Take the time to baste a quilt correctly. It's worth it.

The fun part comes when it's time to remove the basting—that's when you know that your efforts have paid off. There is no greater thrill for a quilter than to finally see the quilted designs without basting stitches complicating and detracting from their appearance.

Here is my preferred method of basting:

One method of basting. I baste my quilts on a floor, using quite a few needles that I have prethreaded with bright, contrasting colors in lengths of about three or four feet each.

I do my basting in parallel rows, first horizontally and then vertically, across the full width and length of the quilt. I start the first row of horizonal basting about 4″ down from the top of the quilt and the first vertical row about 4″ in from one side edge. I make the rows in each direction about 3″ to 4″ apart.

As I baste, I carefully roll up the already basted part of the quilt, to prevent bunching.

Avoiding the basting blues. Basting is a boring process, to be sure, but here are some ways I have found to make it seem like less of a chore: Listen to some favorite music while basting; baste with a friend, and enjoy the conversation; break the process down into short sessions—15 minutes apiece or so—and do something else between sessions.

The Quilting Stitch

Quilting consists of short running stitches, taken completely through a sandwich of three layers: the quilt front, the batting, and the backing. (A few projects in this book are quilted through only two layers, however, because they are three-dimensional and offer limited access for quilting.)

Quilting can also be done by machine, but all of my projects are quilted by hand, because I love the traditional look that hand-quilting creates.

I also prefer to see quilting done whenever possible on the lightest color fabric pieces of a project, to allow the darker pieces to remain bold and unbroken. There are no hard and fast rules, though, and your projects should be made in the way that pleases you most.

Here are some tips for successful and neat quilting:

- **Baste before quilting.** Basting properly before quilting large items is a must, to provide stability and to prevent bunching. On small projects, fully basting the item may not be necessary.

- **Use a quilting hoop or frame.** Be sure to stabilize the quilt layers during quilting, using a hoop or frame; see "Basic Equipment," page 8.

- **Hide all knots.** When beginning each new length of thread, make a knot in one end and pull the first stitch through the quilt from back to front. Give the thread a tug, forcing the knot through the backing fabric until it becomes embedded in the batting. The knot will then be hidden inside the quilt and the backing will look as neat as the quilt front.

- **Make tiny stitches.** Between 8 and 12 stitches-per-inch is a realistic quilting goal to aim for.

Quilting Styles

There are a number of different quilting styles. The ones you choose to use are determined by the quilted effects that you want to create.

Single-outline quilting. Single-outline quilting is done ¼″ from a seam or appliqué, along one side of it, following the contour of the stitching line or fabric edge. It can be done on either side of the shape's outline.

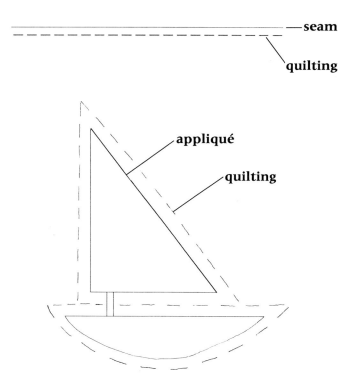

Double-outline quilting. Double-outline quilting is done on both sides of a seam, ¼″ away from it on each side, following the line or contour of the seam.

Quilting in the ditch. Quilting done on top of a seam is called "quilting in the ditch."

Diagonal quilting. Diagonal quilting is done on the diagonal that runs through a patchwork piece, rather than around its outline.

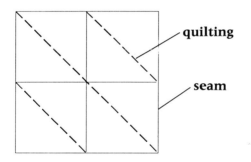

Motif quilting. Quilting a design in a solid unpieced area, such as on a border or in the center of a block, is called motif quilting.

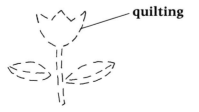

Finishing the Quilt

After assembling and quilting, most projects have raw edges that need to be finished. Bias binding and piping, the most common finishing materials, are discussed in this section. Instructions are also included for hanging a project that is to be displayed on a wall.

Bias Binding

Bias binding is made from strips cut on the bias (the diagonal) of the fabric. Unlike patchwork strips, which are cut on the straight grain of the fabric (see "The Project Elements" on page 20), bias strips are not rectangular in shape. Their long side edges are parallel but are of different lengths. The strips are stitched together, forming one long strip, which is then used for finishing the raw edges of a project.

Bias binding is available in prepackaged form in a variety of colors, but if you want to frame your project with edges that exactly match one of the internal colors or prints, you will have to make the binding, directions for which follow.

Step 1: Mark 1¾″-wide strips on the bias of the fabric (see Marking Diagram).

MARKING DIAGRAM

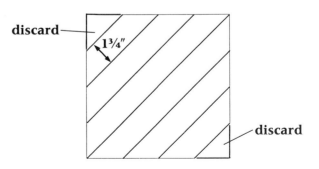

17

Step 2: Trim away the selvage edges of the fabric.

Step 3: Cut out the strips along the marked lines, and discard the small corner pieces.

Step 4: Stitch the strips together, end to end; see Joining Diagrams.

JOINING DIAGRAMS

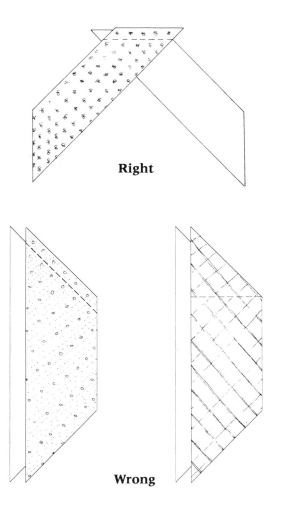

Right

Wrong

Step 5: Press the seams open.

Step 6: Trim away the seam allowance that overhangs the sides of the bias strip, so that both side edges are straight.

Binding the Quilt

Finishing the quilt edges is basically the same procedure with both handmade and purchased binding. Use the following method for binding your quilt, but if you are attaching purchased binding, eliminate any folding and pressing steps that have already been done.

Step 1: Cut a piece of binding the same length as the perimeter of the quilt, plus 2½". Both ends should be cut straight across, not on an angle.

Step 2: Fold and press one long side edge and one end of the binding ¼" to the wrong side.

Step 3: Beginning in the middle of one edge of the quilt with the folded end of the binding, pin the binding around the quilt front, right sides together, matching raw (outer) edges; overlap the ends, tucking remaining end under in the same manner as the first one. Make a tuck in the binding for each corner and pin it to the quilt.

Step 4: Machine-stitch the binding to the quilt ¼" from the outer edge. At each corner, position the needle in the tuck, release the presser foot, and turn the quilt 90 degrees, so that the next quilt edge to be stitched is aligned with the needle. Put the presser foot down again and proceed with the stitching.

Step 5: Fold the binding smoothly to the back of the quilt and pin it in place, covering the stitching line formed in Step 4.

Step 6: Whipstitch the binding to the quilt.

Piping

Piping consists of a cord covered by a fabric strip, the raw side edges of which have been stitched together, to contain the cord and to provide seam allowance for stitching the piping to an item.

Piping can be handmade, but I prefer using the prepackaged type, which comes in a wide enough range of colors to coordinate with any project.

It is most often used for finishing the perimeter of an item, such as a pillow, but piping can also be used to finish individual edges, such as a pocket top. Directions for preparing piping that is to be used around the perimeter of an item follow.

Step 1: Cut a piece of piping the same length as the perimeter of the item, plus 1″.

Step 2: Remove the stitching that secures the fabric around the cord about ¾″ beyond the desired length.

Step 3: Fold back the fabric end and trim away ½″ of cord.

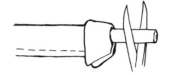

Step 4: Turn the fabric end to the inside, so that the fabric fold is even with the end of the cord.

Step 5: Restitch the fabric along the line where the stitches were removed in Step 2.

Step 6: Prepare the opposite end of the piping, following Steps 1–5, so that the ends will meet smoothly.

Hanging the Quilt

Many projects in this book have been designed to be hung on a wall. Sewing plastic rings (which can be found in crafts shops and hardware stores) to the back of an item is a convenient and inexpensive method of hanging a quilted project. Use picture hooks or small nails attached to the wall for hanging the quilt.

Because the projects are lightweight, I recommend using the lightest weight rings—about ½″ in diameter.

For small projects—up to about 20″ × 20″—three rings are enough. Directions follow for attaching rings to the back of a small quilt. For larger wallhangings, continue dividing and subdividing each half of the quilt with rings until they are spaced about 7″ to 9″ apart.

If any part of your project "pouches out" after it is hung, you may want to sew on additional rings for added support.

Step 1: Sew the first ring to the middle of the backing; take several tiny stitches through the bottom of the ring and the backing fabric only, so that the stitches don't show through on the front of the quilt.

Step 2: Sew a ring to each side of the backing.

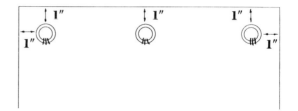

2 All About the Projects

The Project Elements

All projects in this book include a list of supplies that you will need, a cutting guide, and complete directions. I have provided step-by-step directions for the patchwork blocks, as well as actual-size block templates. There are additional actual-size patterns and a number of diagrams, to help you make each project.

I recommend that you read this section and the one that follows (''Templates and Patterns'') before making the projects in Part 3.

The Supplies

All fabric, materials, and amounts needed to make a project are listed as supplies. Materials other than fabric may include batting (for padding flat items), fiberfill (for stuffing pillows), ribbons, lace, piping, or embroidery floss.

Any special tools or equipment not mentioned in Part 1 (see ''Basic Equipment,'' page 7) are also listed as supplies.

Yardages. Most cotton fabrics are 45″ wide, and the fabric yardages listed are based on this width. If the fabric you use isn't 45″ wide, you may have to make some adjustment to the amounts shown, to be sure that you have enough to make the project.

The yardages needed to make the backing and binding are given with other fabrics, although in some cases they are not shown as individual items but are included as part of the total amount needed for all pieces that are to be cut from the same fabric.

The actual sizes needed for the backing, binding, batting, and other project pieces (which may differ from the yardages and amounts listed with the supplies) are given in the cutting guide, information about which follows.

The Cutting Guide

The cutting guide for each project lists all pieces that are to be cut from fabric and other materials. It can be helpful to cut all the pieces ahead of time.

Most pieces are shapes for which templates or patterns are provided. Here are some exceptions.

Strips. In patchwork, strips are rectangular shapes cut on the straight grain of the fabric (not to be confused with bias strips; see ''Finishing the Quilt'' on page 17). Because of space limitations, most additional strips and some squares that aren't part of patchwork blocks are listed by size in the cutting guide, which gives their width, length, and the fabric from which they are to be cut. Seam allowances of ¼″ are included in the measurements—do not add extra seam allowance.

The width of each particular strip will remain constant throughout an individual project, but the length may vary, and all strip lengths are specified.

For example, the cutting guide may list several D strips, all 1½″ wide, that are to be cut, perhaps two 18″ long from one fabric and two 26″ long from another fabric. The strips are two different lengths and two different colors, but all four strips are 1½″ wide and, therefore, D's.

Batting. The batting size listed in the cutting guide is the required size for the project, whether you use a single piece of batting or two lengths pieced together. (For information about piecing batting, see ''The Quilt Layers'' on page 14.)

Backing. As with batting, the dimensions given for the backing in the cutting guide is the size required, whether or not it has to be pieced. (For information about piecing the backing, see "The Quilt Layers" on page 14.)

For smaller projects, such as pillows, the backing is usually the same size as the project's front. For larger projects, such as quilts, the dimensions given provide an extra 2" on each side, to allow for shrinkage during quilting. The excess will be trimmed away after quilting is completed.

Binding. The yardage needed to make the binding for a project is listed with the supplies, and the total length of bias binding needed, whether handmade or purchased, is given in the cutting guide. All lengths have been rounded up to the nearest ¼ yard. (For information about making binding, see "Finishing the Quilt" on page 17.)

Templates & Patterns

Actual-size templates are provided for all patchwork shapes, except for some strips and squares (see "The Project Elements" on page 20). Actual-size patterns for additional shapes, embroidery designs, and quilting motifs are given wherever possible.

Templates

Seam allowances are marked on all templates. For patchwork shapes, the seam allowance is always ¼".

Half-templates. Due to space considerations, half-templates are given for some very large patchwork pieces, which are to be cut from fabric that has been doubled. The edge to be placed on the fabric fold is labeled on each half-template.

Patterns

Seam allowance is included on all patterns for shaped pieces. For most shaped patterns, the seam allowance is ¼", but for some small appliqués, it is only ⅛" and is so marked.

Shaped half-patterns. Half-patterns are given for some overly large shapes, and they are used to cut pieces from doubled fabric. The edge to be placed on the fabric fold is labeled on each half-pattern.

Design half-patterns. Some large embroidery motifs are provided as half-patterns. The center of each motif is clearly labeled. Trace the half-pattern on tissue paper, then make a reverse tracing. Tape together the two tracings to form a complete pattern, matching the center markings.

Enlarging patterns on a grid. Some exceptionally large shapes are provided on a grid and must be enlarged before use.

To enlarge patterns to full size, you can draw a full-size grid by hand, being sure to make the same number of blocks, each the corrected size. Or you can buy premade grid paper from your local fabric store. For 1" grids, I recommend sewing pattern paper, as it is lightweight and inexpensive. For ½" grids, use graph paper, taping pieces of paper together when necessary.

Transposing the patterns is not as difficult as it may appear: Begin by marking dots on the full-size grid wherever pattern lines intersect with grid lines. Sketch the exact shape in each small grid block onto its corresponding full-size grid block—"connecting the dots"—until the entire shape has been copied and enlarged.

Care of Templates and Patterns

If you prepare and store your templates and patterns neatly, using the tips that follow, they will serve you well—and accurately—in your patchwork projects.

Photocopying. I recommend photocopying all templates and patterns before making the projects, to preserve the book. Be sure to go to a high-quality copy shop (don't use the copier at the supermarket or library), because low-quality machines tend to distort lines and can ruin the accuracy of your project. You can find copy shops listed in your telephone directory.

Storage. Templates and patterns should be neatly organized and stored, so that a complete and accurate set will be available whenever you want to use or reuse them.

Gluing a large manila envelope to the inside back cover of this book to hold paper templates and patterns is a good way to keep them organized.

3 The Projects

Attic Window Recipe Holder and Potholder

In my kitchen I have a wonderful antique bookcase, which is made of oak and has a glass front. The bookcase was in sad shape when I first got it, so I had it stripped and rubbed it down with linseed oil, and it now holds my cookbook collection.

I also wanted to have an easily accessible spot to keep loose recipes, especially those that I use frequently. (Some people can memorize all their favorite recipes, but I'm not one of them.) I created the Attic Window Recipe Holder as a place to store my recipes and a quilted piece to decorate another wall in my house.

The recipe holder features a mini block on its pocket, and the coordinating potholder is made from a mini quarter-block. You can make several potholders, some for decorating your kitchen and some for handling hot pots and dishes.

◆◆◆◆◆◆

Mini block: 6″ × 6″
Mini quarter-block: 3″ × 3″
Full-size block: 12″ × 12″
Recipe holder: 9″ × 12″, plus hanger
Potholder: 8″ × 8″, plus hanging loop
Seam allowance: ¼″

◆◆◆◆◆◆

SUPPLIES
(for recipe holder and one potholder)

Fabric:
  ⅓ yard white solid
    Scrap of light red print
    Scrap of dark red print #1
  ½ yard dark red print #2
  ½ yard dark blue print

Ribbon:
  ½ yard red, ½″ wide
  1 yard dark blue, ½″ wide

Embroidery floss:
  1 skein red

Piping: 1⅓ yards red

Batting: ⅓ yard

CUTTING GUIDE

For Attic Window Block
  A: 16 white solid
     8 light red print
     8 dark blue print
  B: 8 white solid
     4 dark red print #1
     8 dark blue print

For Attic Window Quarter-Block
  A: 4 white solid
     2 light red print
     2 dark blue print

B: 2 white solid
    1 dark red print #1
    2 dark blue print

Additional Pieces for Recipe Holder
C (1¾"-wide strip):
    2 dark red print #2, 6½"
    2 dark red print #2, 9"
D (9"×9"): 1 white solid
E (9"×12"): 2 white solid
Piping: 9"
Ribbon: 15" red
Batting: 9"×8¾"
        9"×12"
Binding: 1¼ yards dark red print #2

Additional Pieces for Potholder
C (1¾"-wide strip):
    2 dark red print #2, 3½"
    2 dark red print #2, 6"
    2 dark blue print, 6"
    2 dark blue print, 8½"
Piping: 35"
Ribbon: 3" red
Backing: 8½"×8½" white solid
Batting: 8"×8"

DIRECTIONS

Recipe Holder

Make one mini Attic Window block, following step-by-step directions on opposite page.

For pocket: Stitch shorter C's to top and bottom edges of block; stitch longer C's to sides, completing pocket front.

Baste piping to top edge of pocket front on right side, matching raw edges of piping and patchwork. Pin D to pocket front, right sides together. Stitch top edge of pocket; turn to right side; press. Insert smaller batting piece between pocket front and D; baste all around, to secure batting.

Baste pocket for quilting; see "Quilting" on page 15. Quilt outlines of white A's and B's; quilt inner edge of C border.

For recipe holder back: Transfer embroidery pattern for "FAVORITE RECIPES" and circle between words to one E (see "The Quilt Layers," page 14), so that letters are 1" below top fabric edge. Embroider letters with backstitch; fill circle with satin stitch.

Mark a rectangle ⅛" outside "FAVORITE RECIPES." Set together embroidered E, larger batting, and plain E; baste all edges. Quilt on marked lines.

To assemble: Place pocket on top of embroidered E, with bottom and side edges even, as shown in Recipe Holder Diagram; baste in place, leaving top edge open. Bind raw edges all around; see "Finishing the Quilt" on page 17.

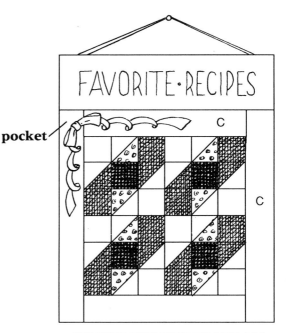

RECIPE HOLDER DIAGRAM

To finish: Tack red ribbon to back of recipe holder; see Ribbon Placement Diagram. Use blue ribbon to make bow, leaving long streamers; curl streamers (see photograph) by hand until you have made three loops. Tack bow in place between loops and at ends as shown.

24

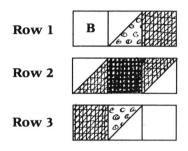

Potholder

Make one mini Attic Window quarter-block, following Steps 1–4 of step-by-step directions.

Stitch red C's and then blue C's to quarter-block as for front of recipe holder pocket, completing potholder front.

To assemble: Fold ribbon in half, to form 1½″ hanging loop; pin to one corner of potholder front on right side, so that cut ends are even with fabric edge and loop faces center. Prepare piping ends; see "Finishing the Quilt" on page 18. Baste piping all around potholder front on right side, matching raw (outer) edges of piping and patchwork.

Stitch potholder front and backing together, leaving 3″ opening in one side for turning; turn to right side. Insert batting through opening, poking it into corners with a knitting needle. Slip-stitch opening closed.

To quilt: Baste and quilt potholder as for recipe holder pocket.

Attic Window Block

Step 1: Sew together a white A and a light A, to form a square. (Make 2 white/light squares.)

Step 2: Sew together a white A and a dark A. (Make 2 white/dark squares.)

Step 3: Stitch pieced and plain squares together, to form three rows.

Row 1   Row 2   Row 3

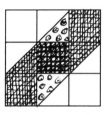

Step 4: Join Rows 1–3, to complete the quarter-block.

Step 5: Make three more quarter-blocks, following Steps 1–4.

Step 6: Join the four quarter-blocks, completing the block.

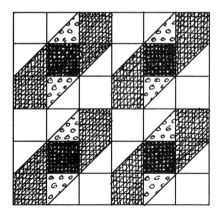

EMBROIDERY PATTERN

FULL-SIZE ATTIC WINDOW BLOCK TEMPLATES

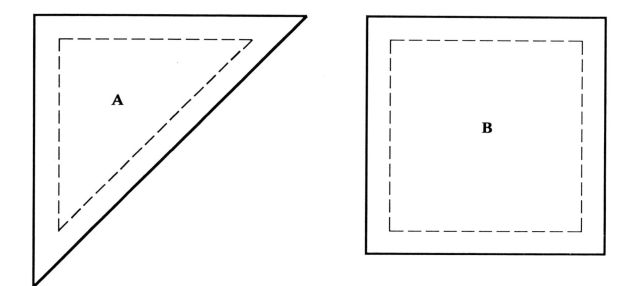

MINI ATTIC WINDOW BLOCK TEMPLATES

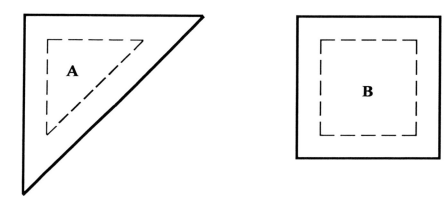

27

Bear Paw Quilt

This project uses a miniature version of a traditional patchwork pattern to make a cheerful child's quilt.

I am fond of teddy bears, and I couldn't resist pairing them with the Bear Paw pattern. I created the block in small form because this quilt is intended for use by small people. Teddy bears represent love and hugs, so I put lots of hearts around the border, and I used the red-white-and-blue color scheme because children love its brightness.

The Bear Paw Quilt can be used as a wall-hanging or as a snuggly crib quilt.

◆◆◆◆◆◆

Mini block: 7″ × 7″
Full-size block: 14″ × 14″
Quilt: 40″ × 48″
Seam allowance: ¼″ (⅛″ for small appliqués)

◆◆◆◆◆◆

SUPPLIES

Fabric:
    2 yards white solid
    ¾ yard medium red print #1
        Scrap of medium red print #2
    ½ yard medium red print #3

    1¾ yards dark blue print #1
    ½ yard dark blue print #2
    ¼ yard light brown print
    1¾ yards desired color, for backing

Embroidery floss:
    1 skein red
    1 skein light brown
    1 skein black

Ribbon: 1¼ yards red, ¹⁄₁₆″ wide

Batting: 1½ yards

CUTTING GUIDE

For Bear Paw Block (make 12)
  A: 16 white solid
       16 dark blue print #1
  B: 4 white solid
       1 medium red print #1
  C: 4 dark blue print #1
  D: 4 white solid

Strips
  E (1½″-wide):
      8 medium red print #1, 7½″
      5 medium red print #1, 25½″
      2 medium red print #1, 33½″
      2 medium red print #1, 40″
      2 medium red print #1, 50″

F (6½"-wide):
    2 white solid, 25½"
    2 white solid, 47½"

Appliqués
Teddy bear: 4 light brown print*
Inner ear: 8 white solid (4 reversed)*
Small heart: 4 medium red print #2
Medium heart: 18 dark blue print #2
Large heart: 14 medium red print #3

Additional Pieces
Ribbon: 4 lengths, 10"
Backing: 44" × 54"
Batting: 40" × 50"
Binding: 5¼ yards dark blue print #1

Seam allowance: ⅛"

QUILT DIAGRAM

DIRECTIONS

Make 12 mini Bear Paw blocks, following step-by-step directions on opposite page.

To assemble quilt front: Stitch three blocks and two 7½" E's together, to form a row; see Row Diagram. Make three more rows in same manner.

Join rows and three 25½" E's; see Quilt Diagram. Stitch two 25½" E's to top and bottom edges of patchwork; stitch 33½" E's to sides.

For inner border, stitch shorter F's to top and bottom patchwork edges; stitch longer F's to sides.

For outer border, stitch 40" E's to top and bottom of piece; stitch 50" E's to sides.

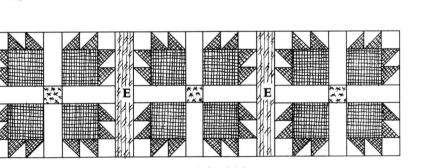

ROW DIAGRAM

To embroider teddy bears: Transfer embroidery details to bears (see "The Quilt Layers," page 14).

Using black floss, work backstitch to outline eyes and to stitch eyebrows and lashes; fill eye centers and noses solidly with satin stitch. Use red to outline mouths with backstitch and to fill tongues with satin stitch. Embroider details on arms and feet with brown backstitch.

To appliqué (see "Appliqué," page 13): Appliqué small hearts (with ¼" seam allowance) and inner ears (with ⅛" seam allowance) on teddy bears where indicated. Tie ribbon bows; tack in place on bears' necks. Appliqué teddy bears (with ⅛" seam allowance) on corners of F border, referring to Quilt Diagram for placement.

Returning to ¼" seam allowance, appliqué large hearts to F border top, bottom, and sides. Appliqué medium hearts in place, overlapping large hearts as shown.

To quilt: Set quilt front, batting, and backing together. Referring to "Quilting" (page 15), baste piece for quilting. Quilt around Bear Paw blocks, teddy bears, large and small hearts, and E strips, as well as the inner and outer edges of F strips.

To finish: Trim backing even with quilt front and batting. Bind quilt edges; see "Finishing the Quilt" on page 17.

Bear Paw Block
◆◆◆◆◆◆◆◆◆◆

Step 1: Sew together a white A and a dark A, to form a square. (Make 4 A/A squares.)

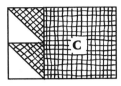

Step 2: Stitch two A/A squares together.

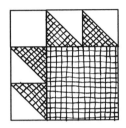

Step 3: Stitch piece from step 2 to a white B.

Step 4: Stitch two A/A squares and a C together.

Step 5: Stitch piece from Step 4 to piece from Step 3, to complete one paw square.

Step 6: Make three more paw squares, following Steps 1–5.

Step 7: Stitch remaining B, D's, and paw squares together, to complete the block.

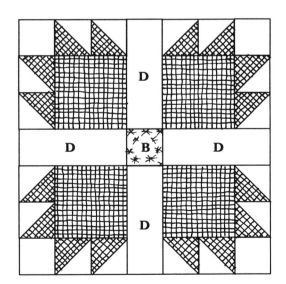

31

APPLIQUÉ PATTERNS

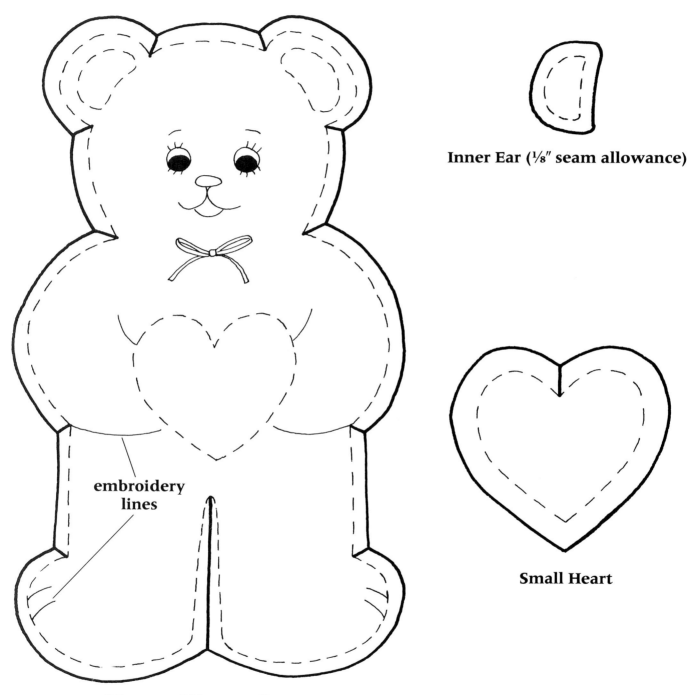

Inner Ear (⅛″ seam allowance)

Small Heart

embroidery
lines

Teddy Bear (⅛″ seam allowance)

32

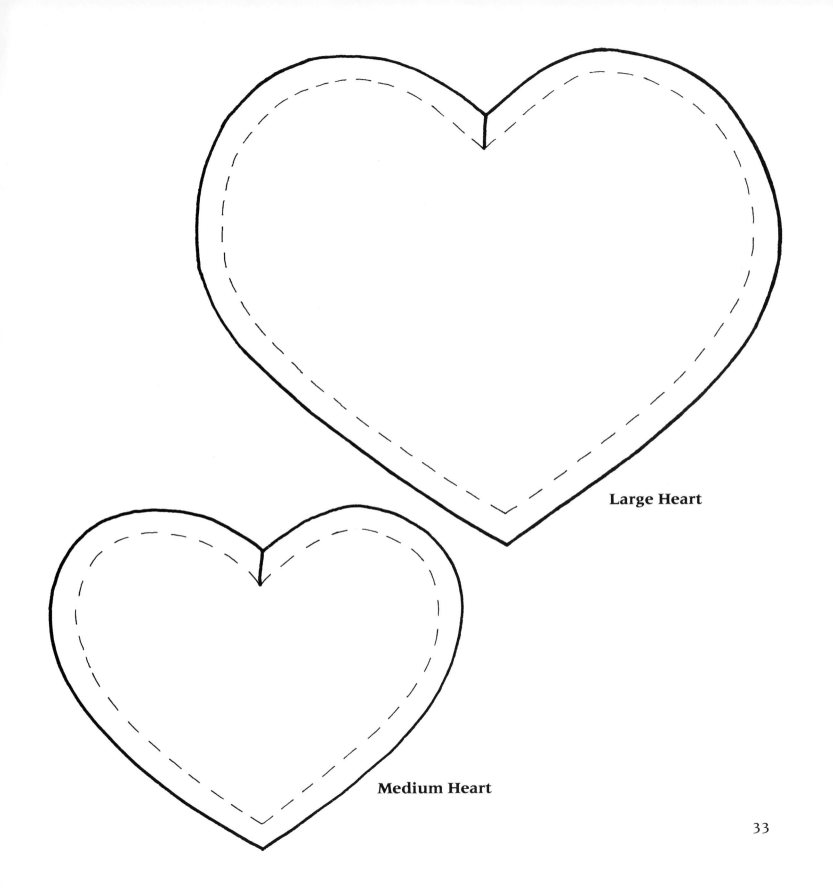

Large Heart

Medium Heart

33

FULL-SIZE BEAR PAW BLOCK TEMPLATES

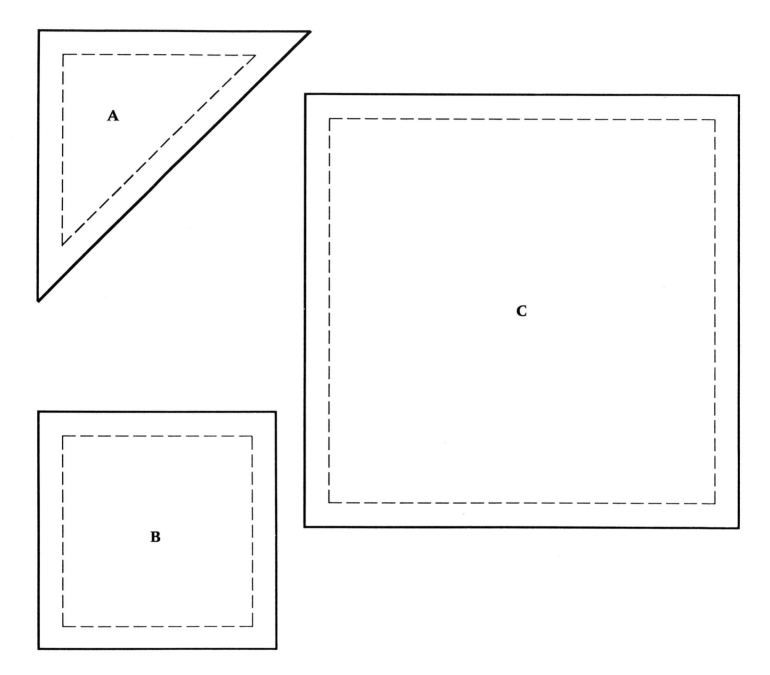

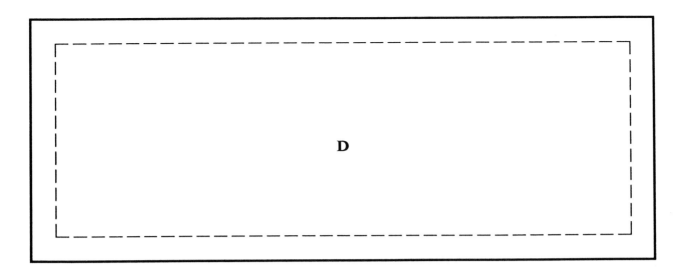

MINI BEAR PAW BLOCK TEMPLATES

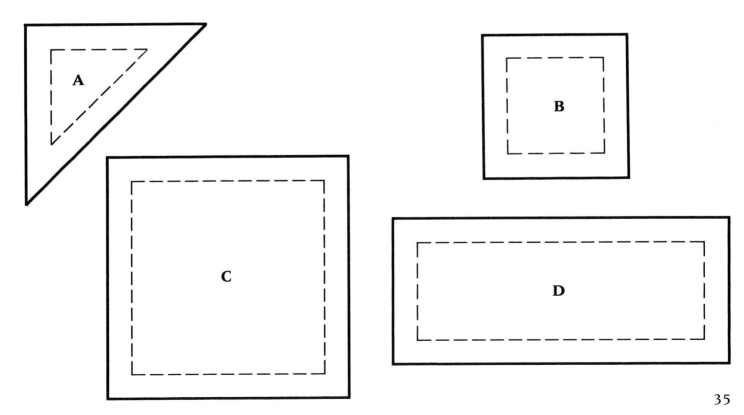

35

Card Trick Hatband

Hats can be such fun to decorate! I once received an invitation for a party to which everyone had been asked to wear clothing that was Victorian in style. After I made my dress, I wanted to complete the look with a huge, outlandish hat typical of that era, so I bought a basic straw hat and loaded it with feathers, stuffed birds, and ribbons. It was a Victorian feast of utter lavishness.

In a way, that is what I have created here—but this hat is a quilter's extravaganza. Mini Card Trick blocks, ribbons, and dried flowers all work together to create a hat that could be worn for a very special event, such as a quilt show.

I hope you have lots of fun as you pull out all the stops making this beautiful and ornate hat.

Mini block: 3" × 3"
Full-size block: 9" × 9"
Seam allowance: ¼"

SUPPLIES

Fabric:
¼ yard off-white solid
Scrap of pale peach print
Scrap of light peach print
Scrap of medium green print
Scrap of dark green print

Ribbon:
4 yards peach, 3" wide
½ yard dark green, 1½" wide

Dried flowers:
5 peach roses
Peach baby's breath

Wide-brimmed straw hat

Glue gun

CUTTING GUIDE

For Card Trick Block (make 4)
A: 4 off-white solid
2 pale peach print
2 light peach print
2 medium green print
2 dark green print
B: 4 off-white solid
2 pale peach print
2 light peach print
2 medium green print
2 dark green print
Backing: 1 off-white solid, 3½" × 3½"

DIRECTIONS

Make four mini Card Trick blocks, following step-by-step directions beginning on page 38.

To assemble block (make 4): Stitch backing to block, right sides together, leaving an opening in one edge for turning; turn to right side. Slip-stitch opening closed.

To decorate hat: Glue ½ yard peach ribbon around crown of hat, so that lower ribbon edge is even with brim. Glue green ribbon over peach ribbon on hat, centering it.

Starting at center front of hat and working around toward back, glue two blocks to each side of center with side corners touching and blocks centered vertically on ribbon (see Hatband Diagram). Glue roses to brim where indicated by asterisks (*) on diagram. Glue on sprigs of baby's breath, filling spaces between blocks and roses; see photograph.

Make decorative bow from remaining peach ribbon as shown or as desired; glue to hat back.

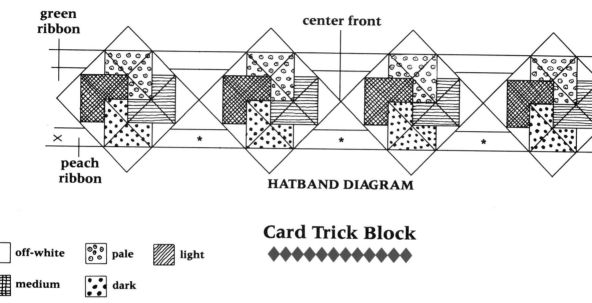

HATBAND DIAGRAM

Card Trick Block

◆◆◆◆◆◆◆◆◆◆◆◆

☐ off-white	⬚ pale ▨ light
▦ medium	⬚ dark

Step 1: Sew together an off-white A and a pale A, to form a square.

Step 2: Sew together an off-white A and a light A.

Step 3: Sew together an off-white A and a medium A.

Step 4: Sew together an off-white A and a dark A.

Step 5: Sew together an off-white B and a medium B, to form a triangle.

Step 6: Stitch a dark A to the piece from Step 5.

Step 7: Stitch a light A, an off-white B, and a dark B together.

Step 8: Stitch a light A, an off-white B, and a pale B together.

Step 9: Stitch a pale A, an off-white B, and a dark B together.

Step 10: Sew together four different colored B's.

Step 11: Stitch pieced squares together, to form three rows.

Row 1

Row 2

Row 3

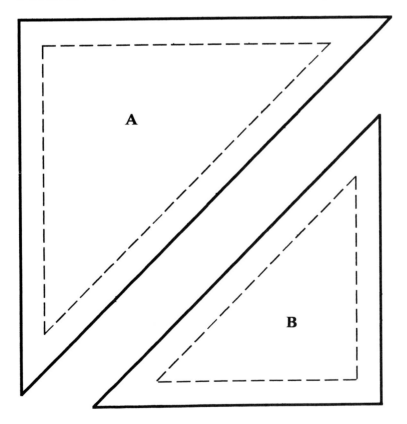

Step 12: Join Rows 1–3, completing the block.

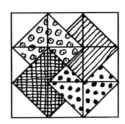

FULL-SIZE CARD TRICK BLOCK TEMPLATES

A

B

MINI CARD TRICK BLOCK TEMPLATES

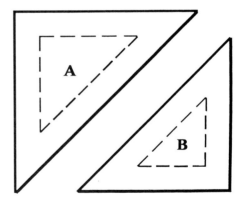

A

B

Ducks and Ducklings Framed Picture

Whenever I travel, I go to all the country shops I can find, to get ideas and make notes for future projects. On a recent trip to Vermont, I visited a small store that carried handcrafted items and found myself drawn to some attractive, individually framed quilt blocks.

My design is a refined version of the framed blocks that I saw there: It uses three mini blocks instead of one full-size one, and a framing mat with three cutouts sets them off. The framed picture can be hung either horizontally or vertically.

Mini block: 5″ × 5″
Full-size block: 10″ × 10″
Framed picture: 20″ × 8″
Seam allowance: ¼″

SUPPLIES

Fabric:
⅛ yard white solid
⅛ yard medium lavender print
⅛ yard dark lavender print
⅛ yard light green print
⅛ yard dark green print

Batting: 20″ × 8″

Wood picture frame: 20″ × 8″

Framing mat: 20″ × 8″

Heavy cardboard backing (if not provided with frame): 20″ × 8″

Small nails or braces (if not provided with frame), for securing cardboard backing

Picture hanger

Tape

CUTTING GUIDE

For Lavender Ducks and Ducklings Block
(make 2)
  A: 12 white solid
       4 medium lavender print
  B: 4 dark lavender print
  C: 4 white solid
       4 light green print
       1 medium lavender print

For Green Ducks and Ducklings Block
  A: 12 white solid
       4 medium lavender print
  B: 4 dark green print
  C: 4 white solid
       4 light green print
       1 medium lavender print

DIRECTIONS

Make one green and two lavender mini Ducks and Ducklings blocks, following step-by-step directions on page 42.

Cut three 5″ × 5″ openings in framing mat, referring to Mat Diagram for placement. Tape blocks behind mat openings as shown in photograph.

Insert mat with mounted patchwork into picture frame. Place batting behind patchwork. Set cardboard backing in place behind batting. Secure backing to frame by pounding small nails or braces into side edges of frame back.

Attach picture hanger to frame back, centering it on top edge.

MAT DIAGRAM

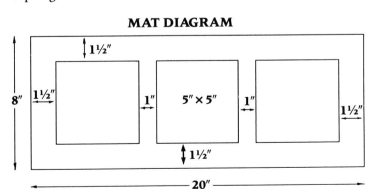

Ducks and Ducklings Block

◆◆◆◆◆◆◆◆◆◆◆◆◆◆◆◆◆◆◆◆◆◆

Step 1: Sew together a white A and a medium A, to form a square. (Make 4 A/A squares.)

Step 2: Stitch two white A's to an A/A square, to form a triangle. (Make 4 triangles.)

Step 3: Stitch a dark B to a triangle from Step 2, to form a square. (Make 4 squares.)

Step 4: Sew together a white C and a light C, to form a rectangle. (Make 4 C/C rectangles.)

Step 5: Stitch rectangles and pieced and plain squares together, to form three rows.

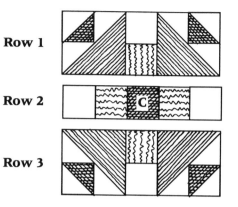

Row 1

Row 2

Row 3

Step 6: Join Rows 1–3, completing the block.

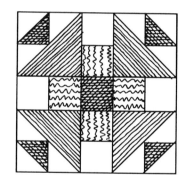

42

FULL-SIZE DUCKS AND DUCKLINGS BLOCK TEMPLATES

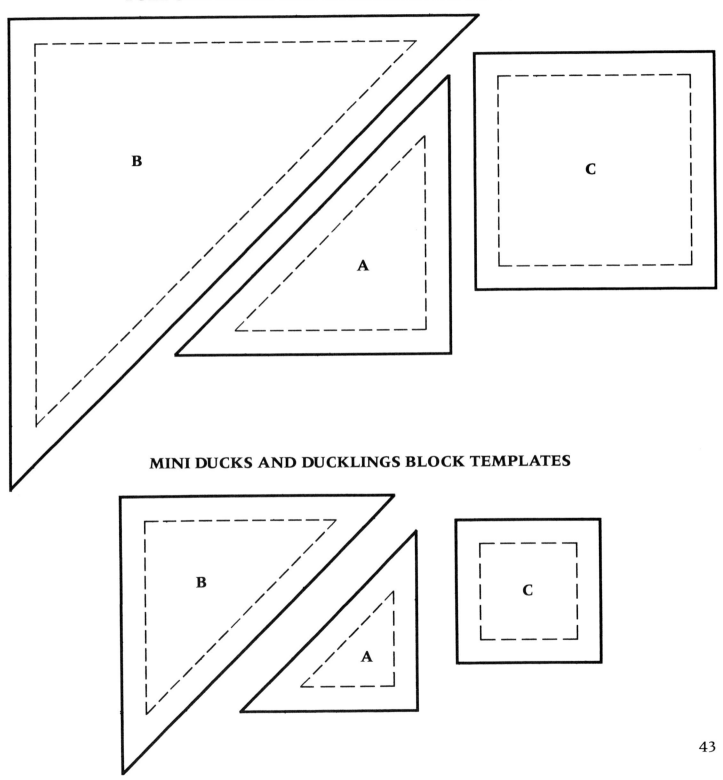

B

A

C

MINI DUCKS AND DUCKLINGS BLOCK TEMPLATES

B

A

C

43

End of Day Basket Cover

Because quilters need a special place to store their special supplies, I have designed this basket cover with a patchwork center to "keep a lid" on your needles, quilting tape, rotary cutter, and other quilting goodies. Small projects-in-progress could also be housed beneath the quilted cover.

The embroidered phrase "QUILTING PROVISIONS" adds a quaint feel to the project for me, because it brings to mind a general store on the prairie and conjures up the image of a woman of the Old West making her monthly trek into town, stopping to buy a needed scrap of calico, a few needles, or some thread to complete a quilt that she has been painstakingly working on.

Your basket with its patchwork cover can stay at home in your work room or go to town—perhaps to a quilting class or club meeting.

Mini block: 6″ × 6″
Full-size block: 12″ × 12″
Cover: at least 13″ diameter, plus lace edging
Seam allowance: ¼″

SUPPLIES

Fabric:
      Scrap of white solid
⅓ yard light white print
      Scrap of bright rust/white print
      Scrap of dark rust solid
      Scrap of medium green print
      Scrap of bright green print
      Scrap of dark green solid

Embroidery floss:
  1 skein dark rust
  1 skein dark green

Cotton eyelet lace: 1½ yards light cream, 1″ wide

Ribbon: 2 yards peach, ½″ wide

Batting: ½ yard

Velcro® dots: 6 of desired color, ⅓″ wide

Round wicker basket: At least 13″ diameter

Instant bonding glue

CUTTING GUIDE

For End of Day Block
  A: 4 white solid
      4 dark rust solid
  B: 4 bright rust print
      4 medium green print (4 reversed)

Additional Pieces
  Leaf:
      4 bright green print (2 reversed)
      4 dark green solid (2 reversed)
  Ribbon: 4 peach, 18″
  Cover*
  Backing*
  Batting*

See Directions for cutting shape.

DIRECTIONS

Make one mini End of Day block, following step-by-step directions on page 46.

For cover shapes: Place a piece of paper larger than basket top over basket top; crease paper, marking outer basket edges all around, including indents for handle (crease will be stitching line). Mark cutting line on paper pattern ¼″ outside creases.

Use cover pattern to cut two cover shapes from light white print (cover and backing) and one shape from batting. Trim away ¼″ seam allowance from batting shape.

For circular motif (see photograph): Transfer "QUILTING" to upper section of cover (see "The Quilt Layers" on page 14), so that center top of lettering is about 5½" from cover center. Transfer "PROVISIONS" to lower section of cover.

Transfer vine pattern to each half of cover, reversing pattern for right half, to complete circular motif.

Work chain stitch to embroider designs, using rust floss for letters and green for vine.

For appliqués (see "Appliqués," page 13): Appliqué leaves along vines, alternating bright and dark green leaves. Appliqué End of Day block inside circular motif, centered.

For lace: Cut lace into two equal lengths, to fit top and bottom edges of cover between handle indents, plus ½". Press lace ends ¼" to wrong side. Stitch lace in place, matching raw (outer) edges.

For ribbons: Pin one end of each ribbon to cover on each side of handle indents, so that they are even with outer edge of cover and loose ends face center. Pin loose ends to cover center, so that they won't get caught in stitching.

For backing: Baste batting shape to wrong side of backing, centered. Stitch cover and backing together, right sides in, leaving 3" opening in bottom edge for turning. Clip into seam allowance of handle indents; turn piece to right side (lace and ribbons will extend beyond cover edges). Remove pins. Slip-stitch opening closed.

For quilting (see "Quilting," page 15): Baste cover for quilting. Quilt around cover edges, patchwork block, vines, and leaves.

For attaching cover to basket: Working along one side of top edge of basket between handles, glue half of three Velcro® dots, evenly spaced, to basket. Glue one half of three more dots to opposite basket edge. Sew other half of dots to corresponding points on cover backing.

Place cover on basket, matching halves of Velcro® dots. Tie ribbons around bases of handles.

End of Day Block

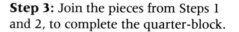

Step 1: Sew together a white A and a bright B, to form a triangle.

Step 2: Sew together a dark A and a medium reversed B, to form a reversed triangle.

Step 3: Join the pieces from Steps 1 and 2, to complete the quarter-block.

Step 4: Make three more quarter-blocks, following Steps 1–3.

Step 5: Join the four quarter-blocks, completing the block.

QUILTING

center

PROVISIONS

center

47

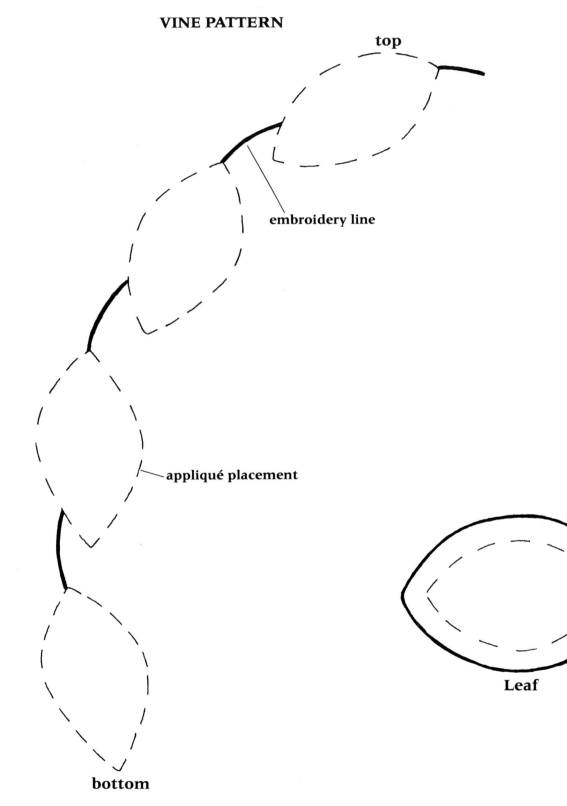

VINE PATTERN

top

embroidery line

appliqué placement

Leaf

48

bottom

FULL-SIZE END OF DAY BLOCK TEMPLATES

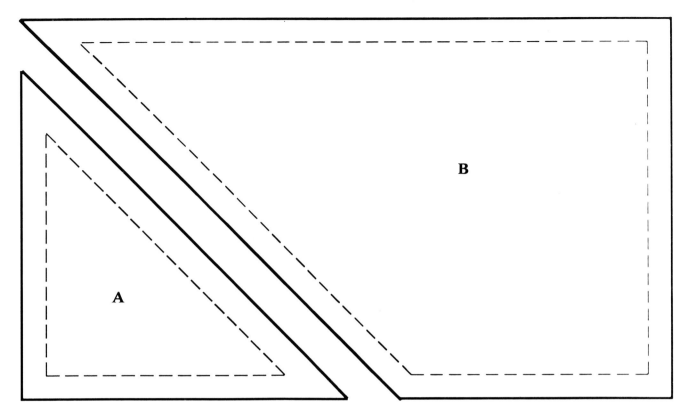

MINI END OF DAY BLOCK TEMPLATES

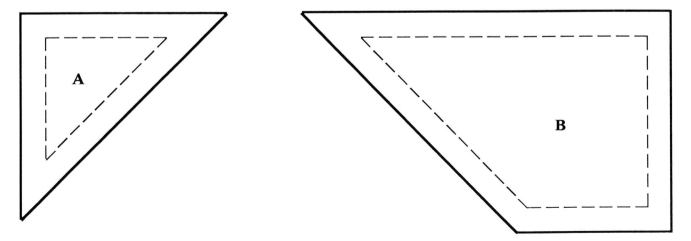

49

Fifty-Four-Forty or Fight Wallhanging

We quilters like to brag about how much we adore quilting. I have seen bumper stickers that announce, "Quilters are the piecemakers" and T-shirts that say, "Quilters put it all together." Just as some sports enthusiasts hang pennants from their favorite teams on the walls of their homes, quilters can display a "pennant" that proclaims their love of their favorite pastime.

This project is a challenging one that incorporates many types of needlework: patchwork, embroidery, appliqué, quilting, and even crazy-quilting. The Fifty-Four-Forty or Fight pattern is a popular one that I have teamed here with the classic Log Cabin pattern and a crazy-quilt heart. In days of old, only lush velvets and satins were used in crazy-quilting, but the heart at the center of this piece is made of ordinary cotton fabric— a modern variation on a traditional technique.

◆◆◆◆◆◆

Mini Fifty-Four-Forty or Fight block: 6″ × 6″
Full-size Fifty-Four-Forty or Fight block: 12″ × 12″
Mini Log Cabin block: 5″ × 5″
Wallhanging: 24½″ × 24½″
Seam allowance: ¼″ (⅛″ for small appliqués)

◆◆◆◆◆◆

SUPPLIES

Fabric:
- 1 yard pale cream print
- ¼ yard pale cream/green print
- ¼ yard light cream/pink print
- ¼ yard medium cream/pink print
- ¼ yard dark cream/pink print
  - Scrap of light cranberry print
- ¾ yard deep cranberry print #1
  - Scrap of deep cranberry print #2
  - Scrap of dark rose solid
- ¼ yard light green print
- ¼ yard medium green print
- ¼ yard dark green print
- ¾ yard desired color, for backing

Embroidery floss:
- 1 skein dark cranberry
- 1 skein medium green
- 1 skein dark green

Batting: ¾ yard

Plastic rings, for hanging

CUTTING GUIDE

For Fifty-Four-Forty or Fight Block (make 4)
- A: 8 deep cranberry print #1
- B: 4 pale cream/green print
- C: 8 pale cream/green print
  - 2 light cranberry print
  - 2 deep cranberry print #2
  - 8 dark green print

For Log Cabin Block (make 8)
C: 1 light cream/pink print*
   1 deep cranberry print #1*
D: 1 light green print
   1 medium green print
E: 1 medium cream/pink print
   1 dark cream/pink print
F: 1 light green print
   1 dark green print
G: 1 light cream/pink print

For Crazy-Quilt Heart Block
I: 1 medium green print
J: 1 medium cream/pink print
K: 1 dark cream/pink print
L: 1 dark green print
M: 1 light green print
N: 1 light cranberry print
O: 1 pale cream print, 12½″ × 12½″
Heart: 1 pale cream print
Tulip: 2 dark rose solid**
Leaf: 4 medium green print**

Additional Pieces
H: 4 pale cream print, 6½″ × 12½″
Backing: 28½″ × 28½″
Batting: 24½″ × 24½″
Binding: 3 yards dark cranberry print #1

Use template C from mini Fifty-Four-Forty or Fight block.

**Seam allowance: ⅛″*

Step 2: Sew light D to piece from Step 1.

Step 3: Sew medium D to piece from Step 2.

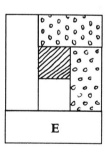

Step 4: Sew medium E to piece from Step 3.

Step 5: Sew dark E to piece from Step 4.

DIRECTIONS

Make four mini Fifty-Four-Forty or Fight blocks, following step-by-step directions on page 56.
   Make eight mini Log Cabin blocks as follows.

Log Cabin Block (make 8)

Step 1: Stitch C's together.

C

Step 6: Sew dark F to piece from Step 5.

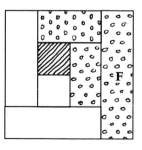

Step 7: Sew light F to piece from Step 6.

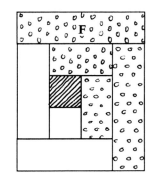

Step 8: Sew light G to piece from Step 7, completing the block.

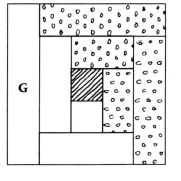

Appliqué two Log Cabin blocks on each H (see "Appliqué" on page 13).

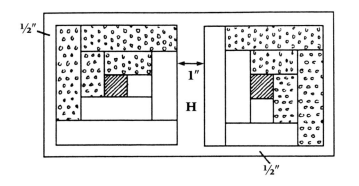

Crazy-Quilt Heart Block

Fold, press, and baste one edge of pieces I, K, L, M, and N ¼″ to wrong side (see patterns for fold lines); do not fold any edges on J. Assemble and baste I, J, K, L, M, and N on heart; see step-by-step directions that follow. Overlap seam allowances of shapes with folded edges as directed; match outer edges of shapes and heart.

Step 1: Overlap top edge of J with bottom (folded) edge of I; baste together.

Step 2: Baste I/J piece in place on heart.

Step 3: Overlap I/J edge with K; baste.

Step 4: Overlap J/K edge with L; baste.

Step 5: Overlap K/L edge with M; baste.

53

Step 6: Overlap K/M edge with N; baste.

Embroider all lapped edges inside heart, using dark green floss and cretan stitch.

For circular motif (see Quilt Front Diagram): Transfer "I'M CRAZY" to upper section of O (see "The Quilt Layers" on page 14), centering placement lines of pattern along top seam allowance of fabric. In similar manner, transfer "ABOUT QUILTING" to lower section of O, centering placement lines along bottom seam allowance. Transfer tulip vine pattern to left side of O; reverse pattern for right side, to complete circular motif.

Embroider words in chain stitch with cranberry floss. Use backstitch and medium green to outline vine. Appliqué tulips and leaves in place along vines with 1/8" seam allowance.

QUILT FRONT DIAGRAM

54

For attaching heart: Press outer edges of heart ¼″ to wrong side. Baste heart to O, centering it within circular motif. Use dark green floss and blanket stitch to secure outer edges of heart in place.

Assembling the Quilt Front

Stitch two Fifty-Four-Forty or Fight blocks to one H, to form quilt top; see Quilt Top Diagram. Stitch two H's to O, to form quilt center; see Quilt Center Diagram. Assemble quilt bottom as for quilt top.

Join quilt top, center, and bottom pieces, referring to Quilt Front Diagram for placement.

Quilting

Transfer quilting motifs to O, above and below heart, and in corners.

Set quilt front, batting, and backing together. Referring to ''Quilting'' (page 15), baste piece for quilting. Quilt marked motifs on O. Quilt around patchwork block outlines.

Finishing

Trim backing even with quilt front and batting. Bind quilt edges; see ''Finishing the Quilt'' on page 17. Attach rings, for hanging.

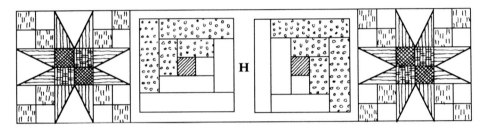

QUILT TOP DIAGRAM

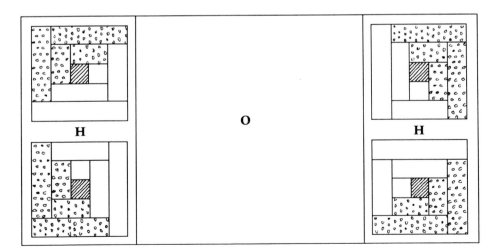

QUILT CENTER DIAGRAM

Fifty-Four-Forty or Fight Block

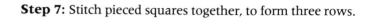

Step 1: Stitch two A's to a B, to form a pale/deep square. (Make 4 pale/deep squares.)

Step 2: Sew together a pale C and a dark C, to form a rectangle. (Make 2 pale/dark rectangles.)

Step 3: Join pieces from Step 2, to form a square.

Step 4: Make three more pale/dark squares, following Steps 2 and 3.

Step 5: Sew together a light C and a deep C, to form a rectangle. (Make 2 light/deep rectangles.)

Step 6: Join pieces from Step 5, to form a square.

Step 7: Stitch pieced squares together, to form three rows.

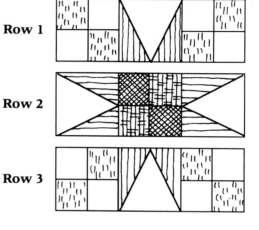

Row 1

Row 2

Row 3

Step 8: Join Rows 1–3, completing the block.

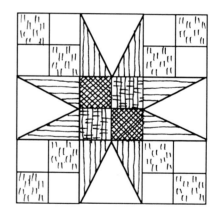

APPLIQUÉ PATTERNS

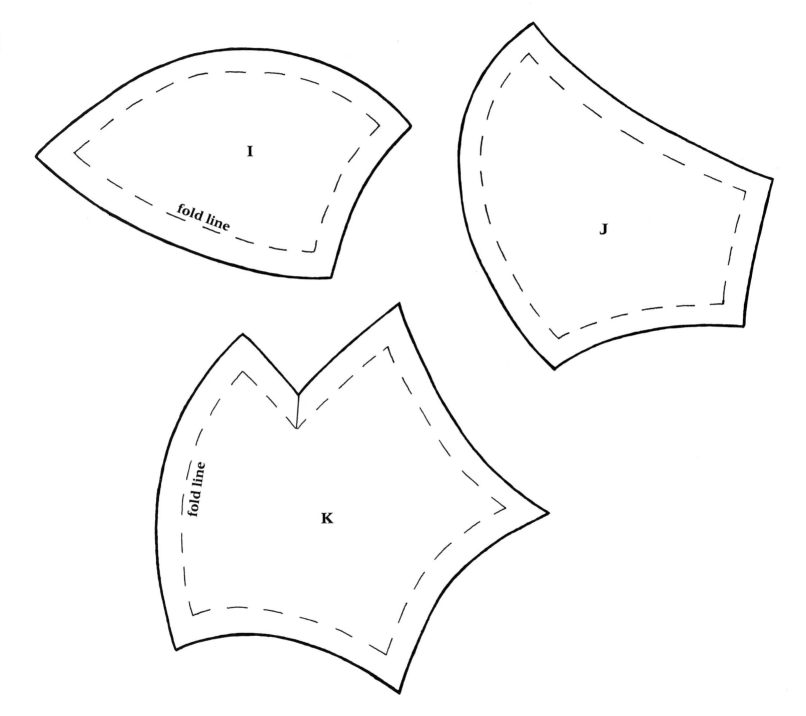

I

fold line

J

fold line

K

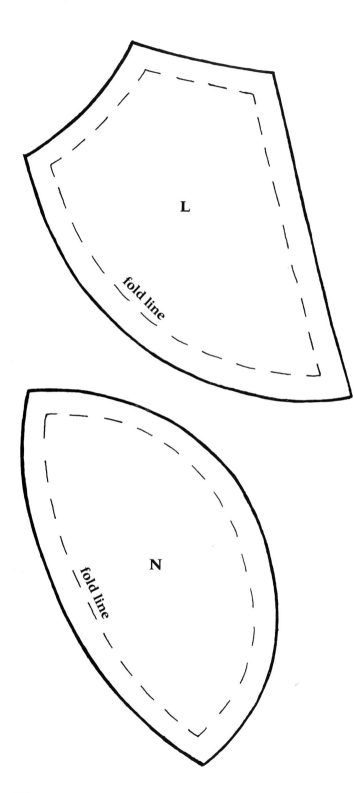

L

fold line

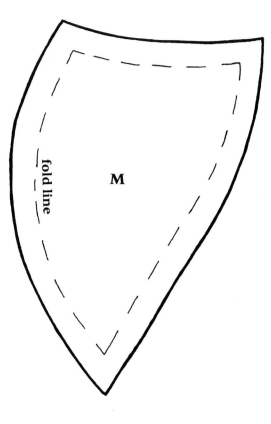

fold line

M

Tulip (⅛″ seam allowance)

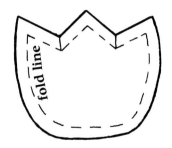

fold line

Leaf (⅛″ seam allowance)

fold line

fold line

N

fold line

Heart

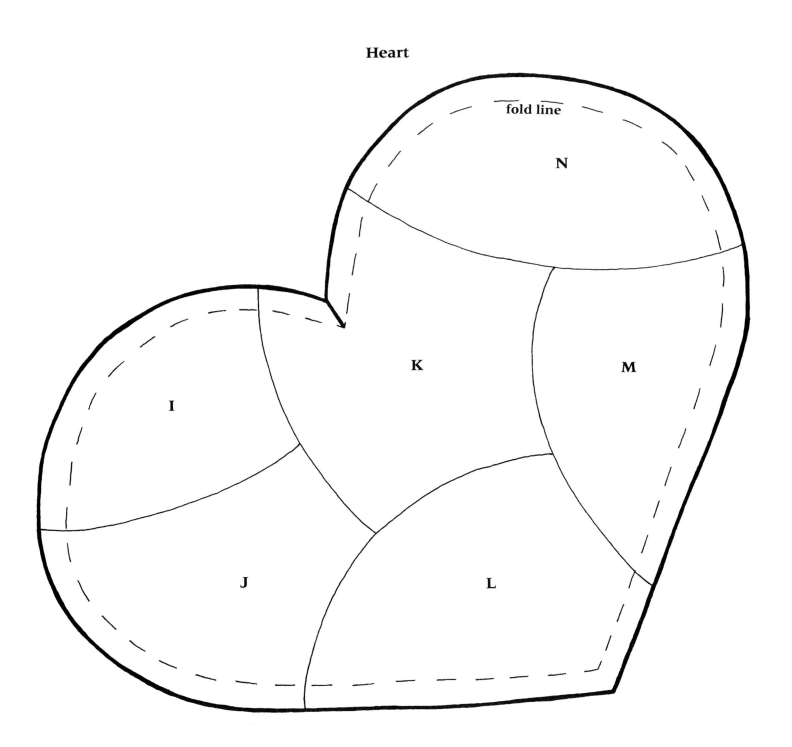

fold line

N

I

K

M

J

L

center

top seam | allowance

I'M CRAZY ABOUT QUILTING

bottom seam allowance | center

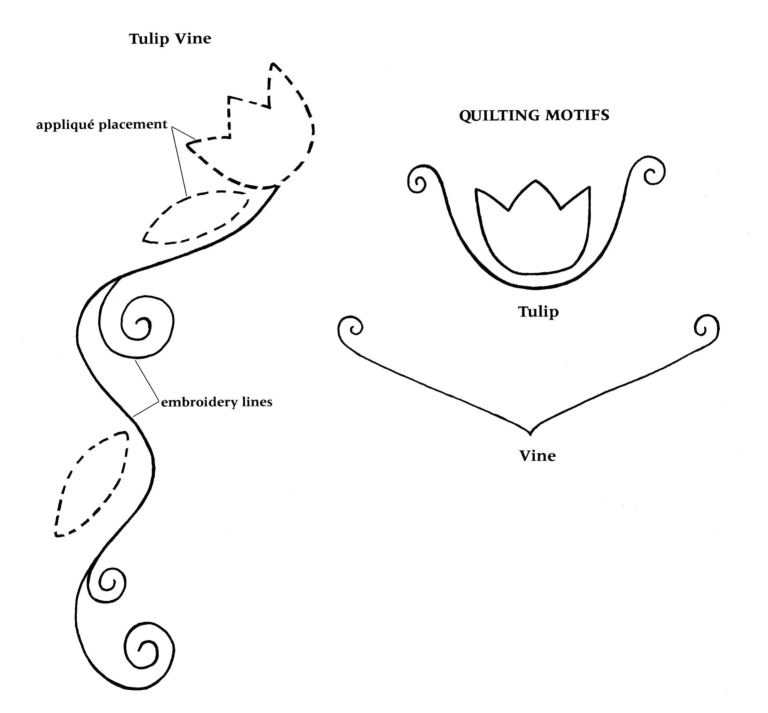

Tulip Vine

appliqué placement

embroidery lines

QUILTING MOTIFS

Tulip

Vine

61

**FULL-SIZE FIFTY-FOUR-FORTY OR FIGHT
BLOCK TEMPLATES**

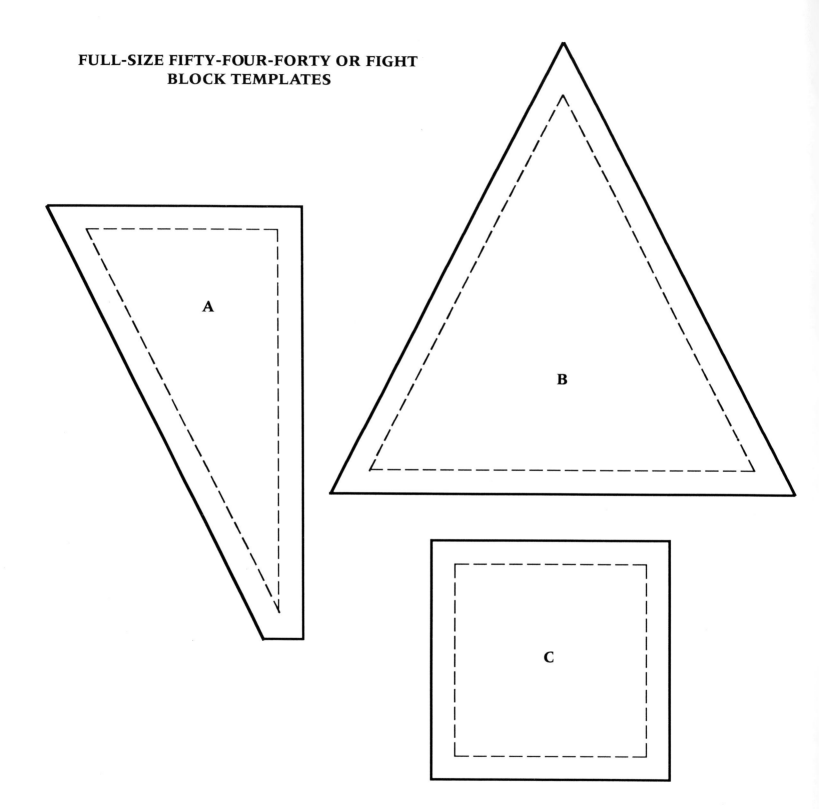

MINI FIFTY-FOUR-FORTY OR
FIGHT BLOCK TEMPLATES

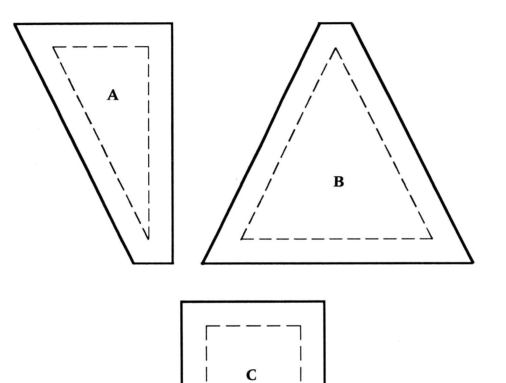

MINI LOG CABIN BLOCK TEMPLATES

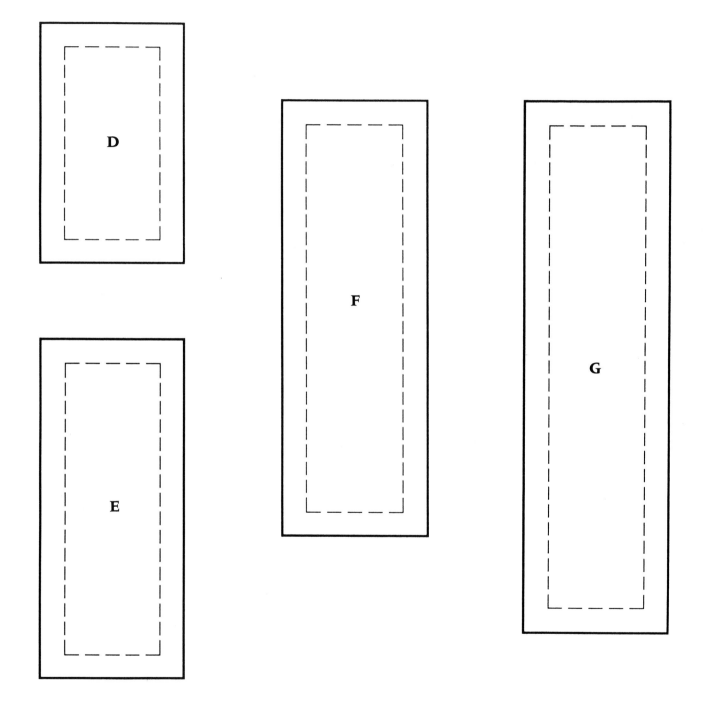

Grape Basket Quilt

A friend of mine has an extensive collection of baskets, most of which she has made. She gathers reeds and vines, then soaks and weaves them into interesting shapes. Basketmaking seems like a difficult craft to me and, as much as I adore baskets, I don't think that I could ever get the hang of making them the way my friend does. Still, in my own way I am a basketmaker—mine are made of fabric and take the form of patchwork.

For this project I used the Grape Basket pattern. Unlike some basket blocks that are quite complicated, this is a relatively simple one that works up quickly. The triangles that fill out the center of the piece have a quilted grape-cluster motif, and purple fabrics further carry out the grape theme.

Full-size block: 10″ × 10″
Quilt: 67½″ × 67½″
Seam allowance: ¼″

SUPPLIES

Fabric:
  1½ yards white solid
  ½ yard light purple solid #1
  ½ yard light purple solid #2
  1 yard medium purple print #1
  1 yard medium purple print #2
  1½ yards dark purple print
    Scrap of medium orchid solid
  1⅓ yards light brown solid
  4 yards desired color, for backing

Batting: 4 yards

CUTTING GUIDE

For Grape Basket Block (make 13)
  A: 13 white solid
      8 medium purple print #1
      3 dark purple print
      2 light brown solid
  B: 1 white solid
      1 light brown solid
  C: 8 white solid

For Border Block (make 4)
  A: 4 white solid*
      2 medium orchid solid*
      2 dark purple print*

Additional Pieces
  D (2½″-wide strip):
      2 light purple solid #1, 63½″
      4 light purple solid #2, 63½″
      2 light purple solid #2, 67½″
      4 medium purple print #1, 63½″
      18 medium purple print #2, 10½″

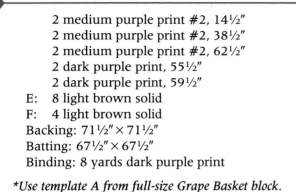

2 medium purple print #2, 14½"
2 medium purple print #2, 38½"
2 medium purple print #2, 62½"
2 dark purple print, 55½"
2 dark purple print, 59½"
E: 8 light brown solid
F: 4 light brown solid
Backing: 71½" × 71½"
Batting: 67½" × 67½"
Binding: 8 yards dark purple print

Use template A from full-size Grape Basket block.

DIRECTIONS

Make 13 full-size Grape Basket blocks, following step-by-step directions on page 70.

Make four mini border blocks as follows.

Border Block (make 4)

Step 1: Sew together a white A and a dark A, to form a square. (Make 2 white/dark squares.)

Step 2: Sew together a white A and a medium A. (Make 2 white/medium squares.)

Step 3: Stitch a white/dark square and a white/medium square together, to form a rectangle. (Make 2 rectangles.)

Step 4: Join pieces from Step 3, completing the block.

ROW DIAGRAM

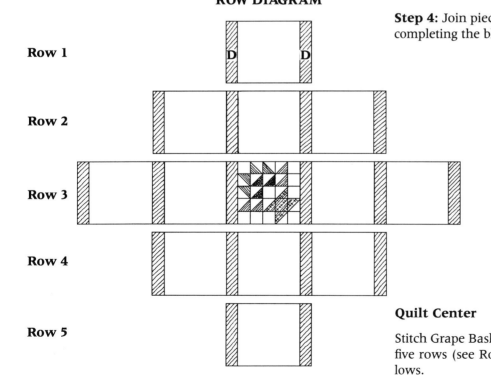

Row 1

Row 2

Row 3

Row 4

Row 5

Quilt Center

Stitch Grape Basket blocks and 10½" D's together, to form five rows (see Row Diagram). Complete each row as follows.

Step 1: Stitch 14½" D to Row 1. Attach an E and then two F's, completing Row 1.

Step 2: Stitch 38½" D to Row 2; stich F's to sides, completing Row 2.

Step 3: Stitch 62½" D's to Row 3; stitch E's to sides, completing Row 3.

Step 4: Repeat Step 2, to complete Row 4.

Step 5: Repeat Step 1, to complete Row 5.

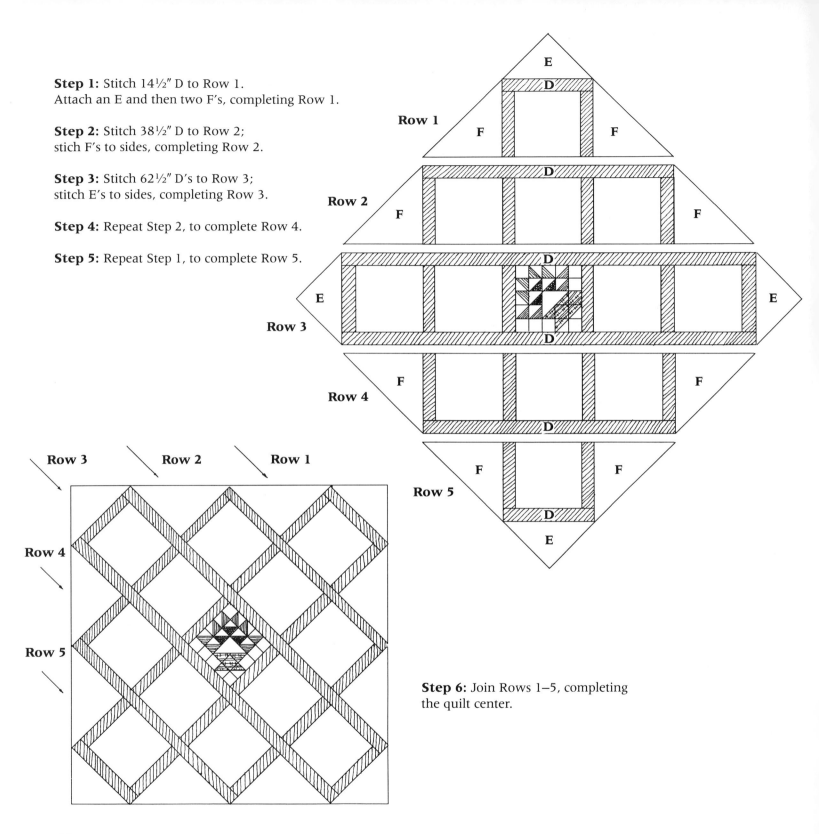

Step 6: Join Rows 1–5, completing the quilt center.

Borders

Add three borders as follows (see Quilt Diagram).

Inner border: Stitch 55½" dark purple D's to top and bottom edges of quilt center. Stitch 59½" dark purple D's to sides.

Middle border: Sew together one 63½" light (light purple #1) D and one 63½" medium (medium purple) D, side by side, to form light/medium D/D border strip. Make three more light/medium D/D's. Stitch border blocks to ends of two D/D's. Stitch shorter D/D's to patchwork top and bottom. Stitch longer D/D's to sides.

Outer border: Stitch 63½" light (light purple #2) D's to top and bottom of patchwork. Stitch 67½" light (light purple #2) D's to sides.

Quilting

Transfer grape cluster and Methodist fan motifs to quilt front (see "The Quilt Layers," page 14), referring to Quilt Diagram for placement: Mark cluster top on E's; mark complete cluster on F's. Mark fan pattern on striped borders as shown.

Set quilt front, batting, and backing together. Referring to "Quilting" (page 15), baste piece for quilting. Quilt marked motifs, and quilt around basket blocks.

Finishing

Trim backing even with quilt front and batting. Bind quilt edges; see "Finishing the Quilt" on page 17.

QUILT DIAGRAM

69

Grape Basket Block

Step 1: Sew together a white A and a medium A, to form a square. (Make 8 white/medium A/A squares.)

Step 2: Sew together a white A and a dark A. Make 3 white/dark A/A squares.)

Step 3: Sew together a white A and a light A. (Make 2 white/light A/A squares.)

Step 4: Sew B's together, to form a square.

Step 5: Stitch A/A's and C's together, to form Rows 1, 2, and 5.

Step 6: Stitch together three white/medium A/A squares and a white/dark A/A square, to form left section of combined Rows 3 and 4.

Step 7: Sew together a white/light A/A square and a C, to form right section of Rows 3 and 4.

Step 8: Join B/B and pieces from Steps 6 and 7, to complete Rows 3 and 4.

Step 9: Join Rows 1–5, completing the block.

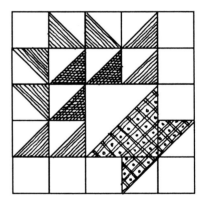

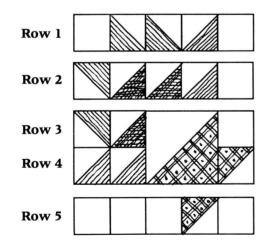

Row 1
Row 2
Row 3
Row 4
Row 5

70

Grape Cluster

cluster top

cluster bottom

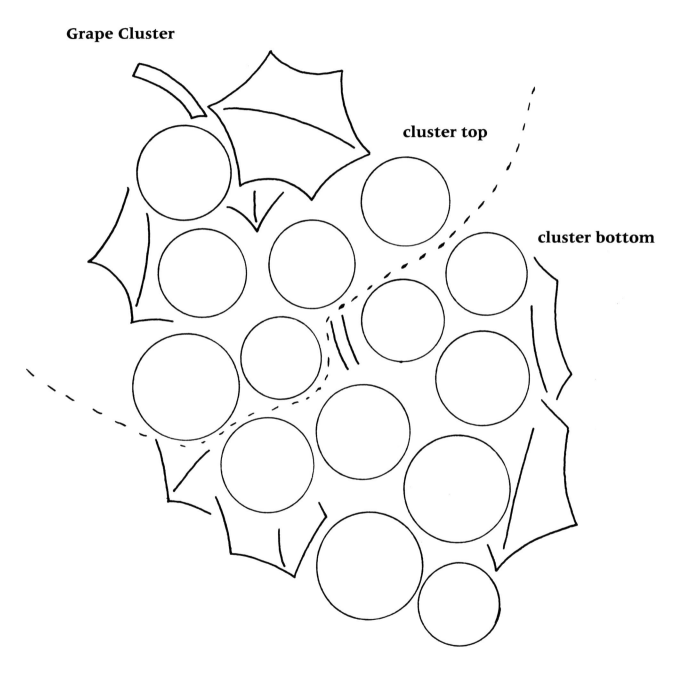

Methodist Fan

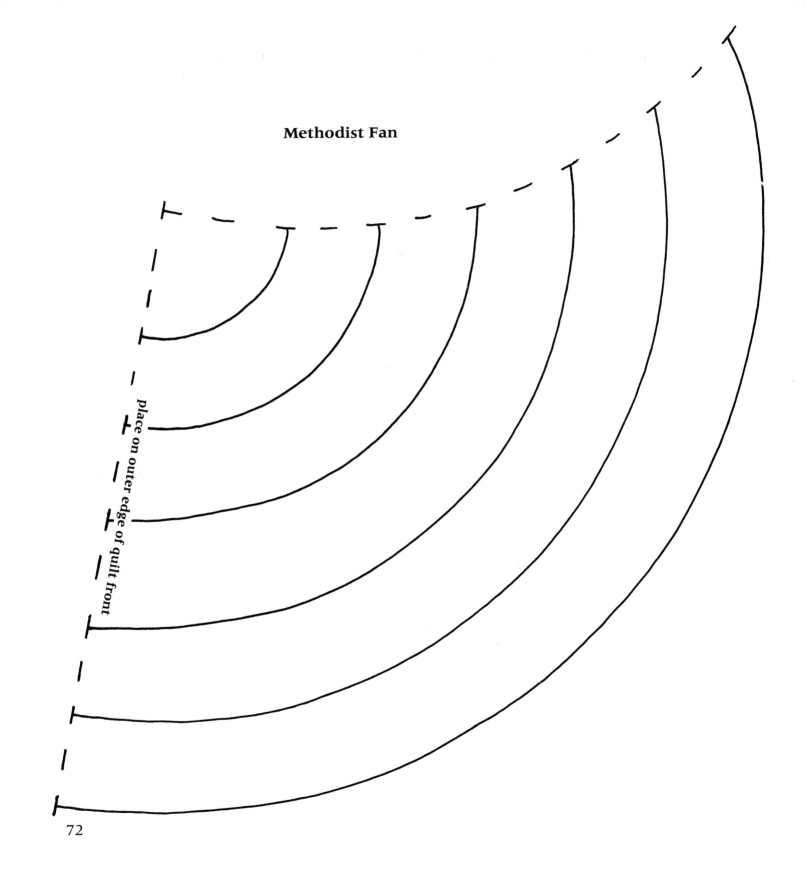

place on outer edge of quilt front

72

TRIANGLE TEMPLATES

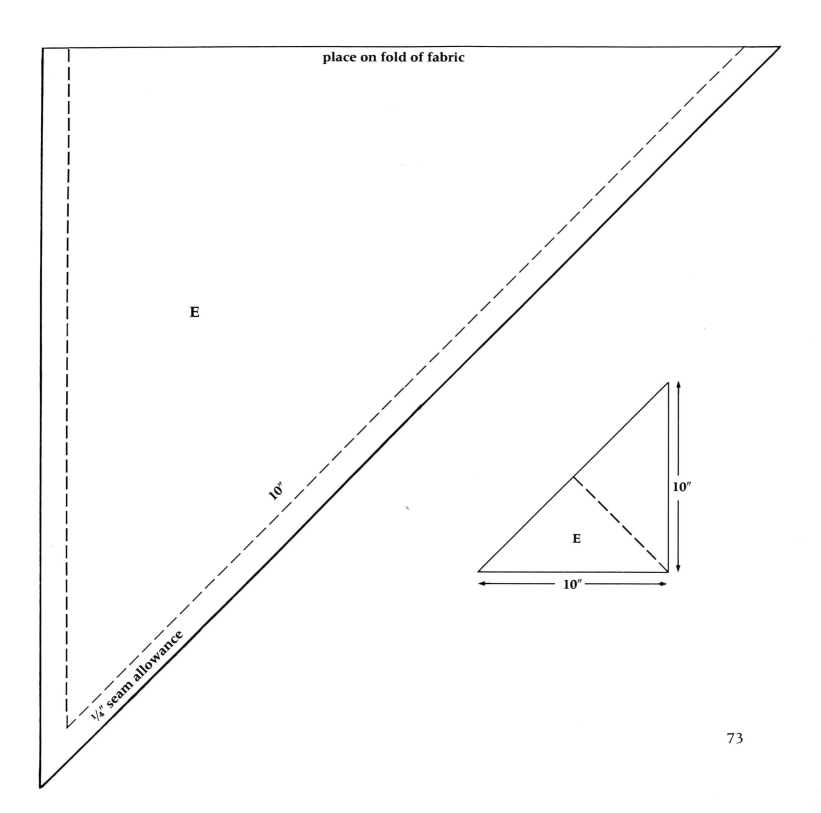

place on fold of fabric

E

10"

¼" seam allowance

10"

E

10"

10"

73

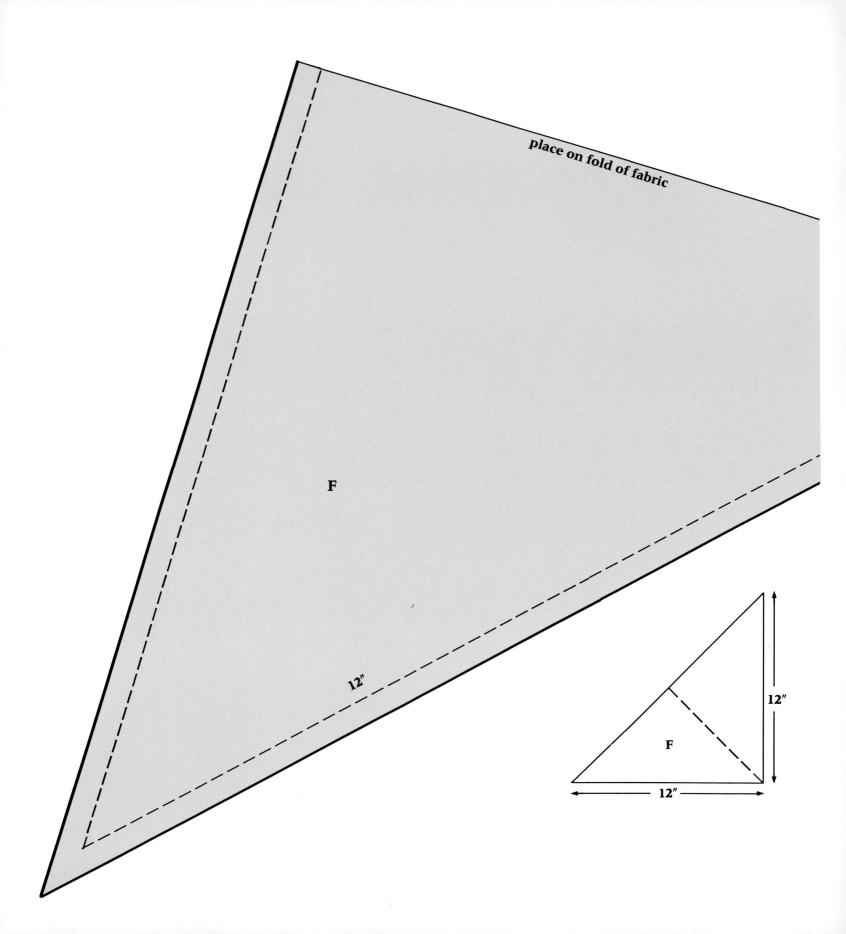

place on fold of fabric

F

12"

12"

12"

F

12"

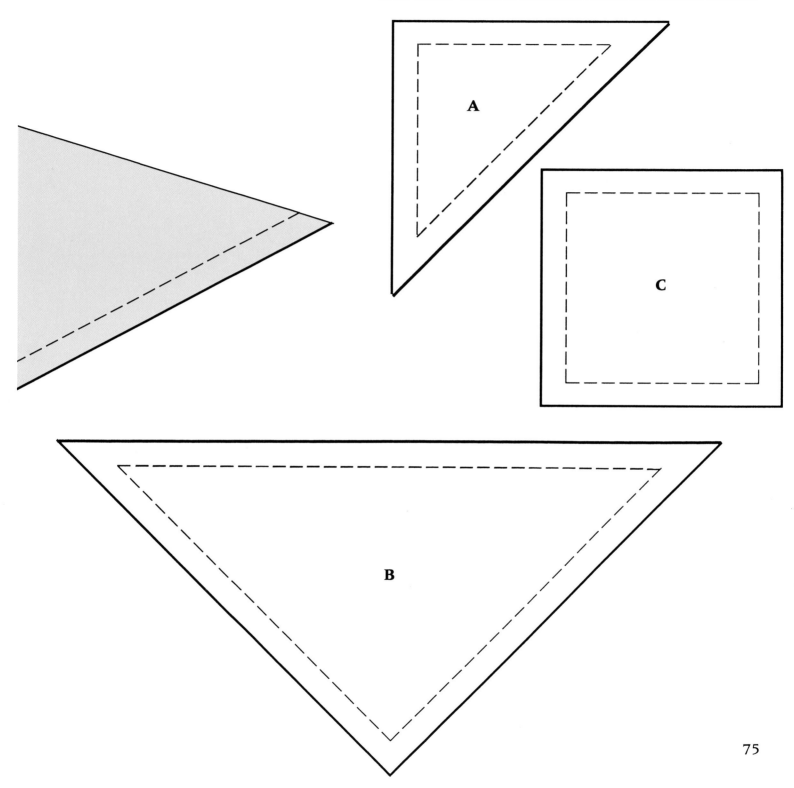

A

C

B

75

Heart and Home Wallhanging

Two of my favorite motifs are the heart and the home, which represent warmth, love, and good feelings. The Heart and Home Wallhanging has lots of both, with berry-and-leaf vines completing the design.

I originally pictured this piece in red, white, and blue. But when I shopped for fabric with Carol Porter (who made the sample for this project), we couldn't find the particular red that I had in mind, so we decided to use cranberry, gray, and black instead. It's an unusual color scheme for me, but I am pleased with the results and feel that the colors work well together.

Carol thinks so too. She loved the wallhanging so much that I gave her the sample to keep. She is redecorating her kitchen and has decided to use this piece for the main theme of her room. She plans to use the small home, berry, and vine patterns to stencil along the top edges of her kitchen walls. I am looking forward to seeing her newly decorated kitchen, the idea for which came from this project.

◆◆◆◆◆◆

Full-size Home block: 12″ × 12″
Mini Home block: 5″ × 5″
Mini nine-patch: 3″ × 3″
Mini letter blocks: 5″ × 5″
Wallhanging: 33″ × 38″
Seam allowance: ¼″ (⅛″ for small appliqués)

◆◆◆◆◆◆

SUPPLIES

Fabric:
- ½ yard muslin solid
- ¼ yard light cream print
  Scrap of medium cream print
- ⅛ yard dark cream print
- ⅛ yard light/dark cream striped
- ¼ yard medium cranberry print
- ¼ yard dark cranberry print #1
- ¼ yard dark cranberry print #2
- ¼ yard dark cranberry print #3
- ¼ yard dark cranberry print #4
  Scrap of dark green solid
- ⅓ yard dark gray print
  Scrap of dark blue-gray print
- 1¼ yards black print
- 1¼ yards desired color, for backing

Embroidery floss:
- 1 skein bright cranberry
- 1 skein dark green

Batting: 1 yard

Plastic rings, for hanging

CUTTING GUIDE

For Full-Size Home Block

A: 1 muslin solid
B: 2 dark cranberry print #4
C: 2 medium cream print (1 reversed)
D: 2 muslin solid (1 reversed)
E: 2 medium cranberry print (1 reversed)
F: 1 dark gray print
G: 1 dark gray print
H: 2 muslin solid
I: 1 black print
J: 2 muslin solid

For Letter Blocks

Refer to Patchwork Alphabet Quilt (page 199). Follow Cutting Guide for four each of mini blocks "H" and "E" and for two each of "A," "R," "T," "O," and "M": Cut all white solid pieces from muslin solid. Cut all nonwhite pieces from medium cranberry print and assorted dark cranberry prints; use one print for all pieces of each individual block.

For Nine-Patch (make 10)

K: 4 light cream print
    4 dark cream print
    1 dark cranberry print #3

For Mini Home Block (make 2)

P: 2 light cream print
Q: 1 dark blue-gray print
R: 1 dark cranberry print #4
S: 1 dark blue-gray print
T: 1 black print

Additional Pieces

L: 10 light/dark cream striped
M (3"-wide strip):
    2 muslin solid, 18½"
N (1½"-wide strip):
    2 black print, 18½"
    2 black print, 25½"
O: 4 light cream print
U (1¾"-wide strip):
    2 black print, 30½"
    2 black print, 38"

Small heart:
    5 medium cranberry print
    5 dark cranberry print #2
Large heart: 2 dark cranberry print #3
Leaf: 34 dark green solid*
Backing: 37" × 42"
Batting: 33" × 38"
Binding: 4¼ yards black print

Seam allowance: ⅛"

DIRECTIONS

Make one full-size Home block, following step-by-step directions on page 80.

Make four each of mini blocks "H" and "E," plus two each of "A," "R," "T," "O," and "M"; see Patchwork Alphabet Quilt.

Make ten mini nine-patches and two mini Home blocks as follows.

Nine-Patch (make 10)

Step 1: Stitch K's together, to form three rows.

Row 1
Row 2
Row 3

Step 2: Join Rows 1–3, completing the block.

Mini Home Block (make 2)

Step 1: Appliqué P's (windows) on Q (home side).

Step 2: Appliqué R (door) on S (home front).

Step 3: Appliqué Q, S, and T (roof) on an O; see Quilt Diagram for placement.

Additional Appliqués and Embroidery

Appliqué small hearts on L's. Appliqué large hearts on two O's.

Transfer embroidery pattern for vine and berries to M's (see "The Quilt Layers," page 14), centering motif on each piece. Work vines in backstitch with green floss; fill berries in satin stitch with cranberry. Appliqué leaves along vines with ⅛" seam allowance.

Assembling the Quilt Front

Arrange nine-patches and L's on work surface, referring to Quilt Diagram for placement; alternate medium and dark hearts as shown. Sew together center four blocks of top row, to form four-block strip. Sew together center four blocks of bottom row in same manner. Sew together six-block sides. Stitch four-block strips to full-size Home block; stitch six-block strips to sides.

Stitch M's to top and bottom patchwork edges. Stitch shorter N's to top and bottom of piece; stitch longer N's to sides.

For outer borders: Stitch letter blocks together, to form two "HEART" and two "HOME" strips; see Quilt Diagram. Stitch O's to ends of "HEART" strips. Stitch "HOME" strips to top and bottom edges of patchwork; stitch "HEART" strips to sides.

Stitch shorter U's to top and bottom of piece; sew longer U's to sides.

Quilting

Set quilt front, batting, and backing together. Referring to "Quilting" (page 15), baste piece for quilting. Outline-quilt on all blocks and around all appliqué designs and patchwork letters.

Finishing

Trim backing even with quilt front and batting. Bind quilt edges; see "Finishing the Quilt" on page 17. Attach rings for hanging.

QUILT DIAGRAM

Home Block

♦♦♦♦♦♦♦♦

Step 1: Appliqué B's (chimneys) and C's (smoke) on A, to form Row 1.

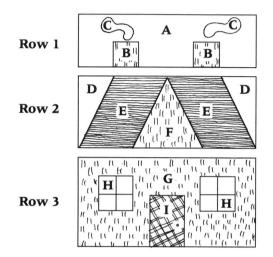

Step 2: Stitch D's, E's, and F together, to form Row 2.

Step 3: Appliqué H's (windows) and I (door) on G, to form Row 3.

Step 4: Use cranberry floss to separate windows into four panes each with lines of backstitch; fill doorknob with satin stitch.

Step 5: Join Rows 1–3.

Step 6: Stitch J's to sides, completing the block.

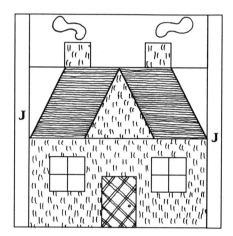

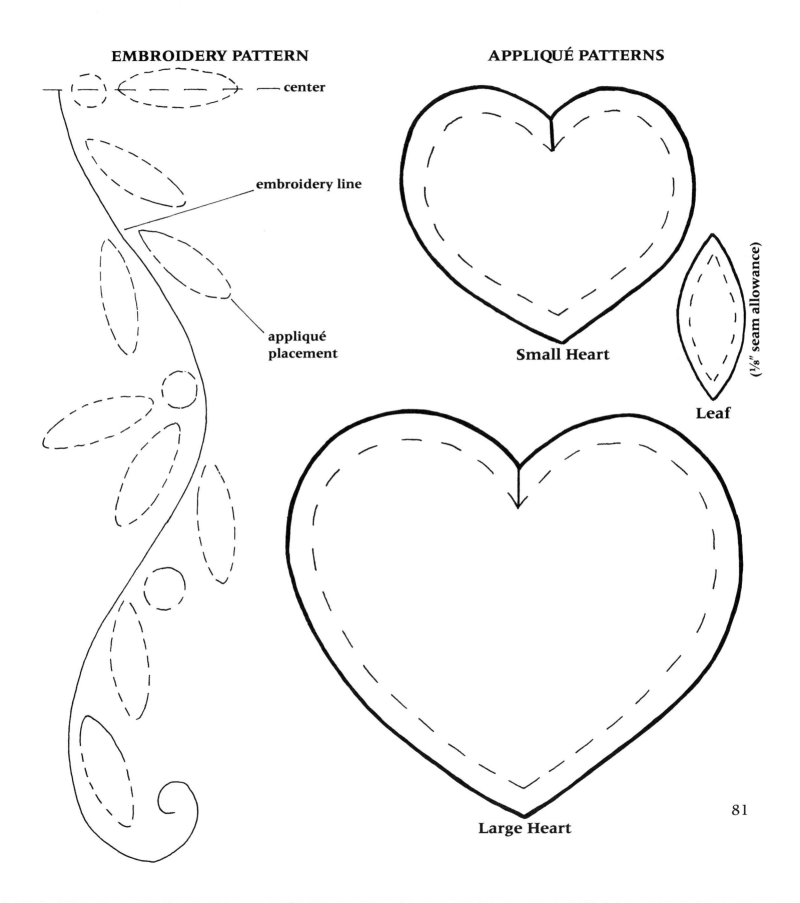

EMBROIDERY PATTERN

center

embroidery line

appliqué placement

APPLIQUÉ PATTERNS

Small Heart

Leaf

(⅛" seam allowance)

Large Heart

81

NINE-PATCH TEMPLATE

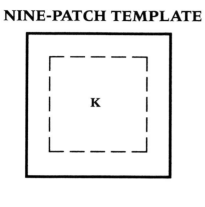

K

SMALL HEART BLOCK TEMPLATE

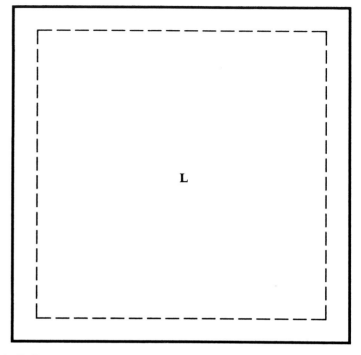

L

FULL-SIZE HOME BLOCK TEMPLATES

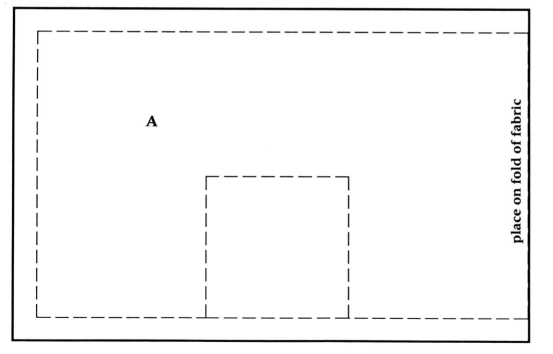

A

place on fold of fabric

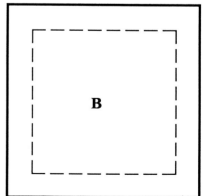

B

82

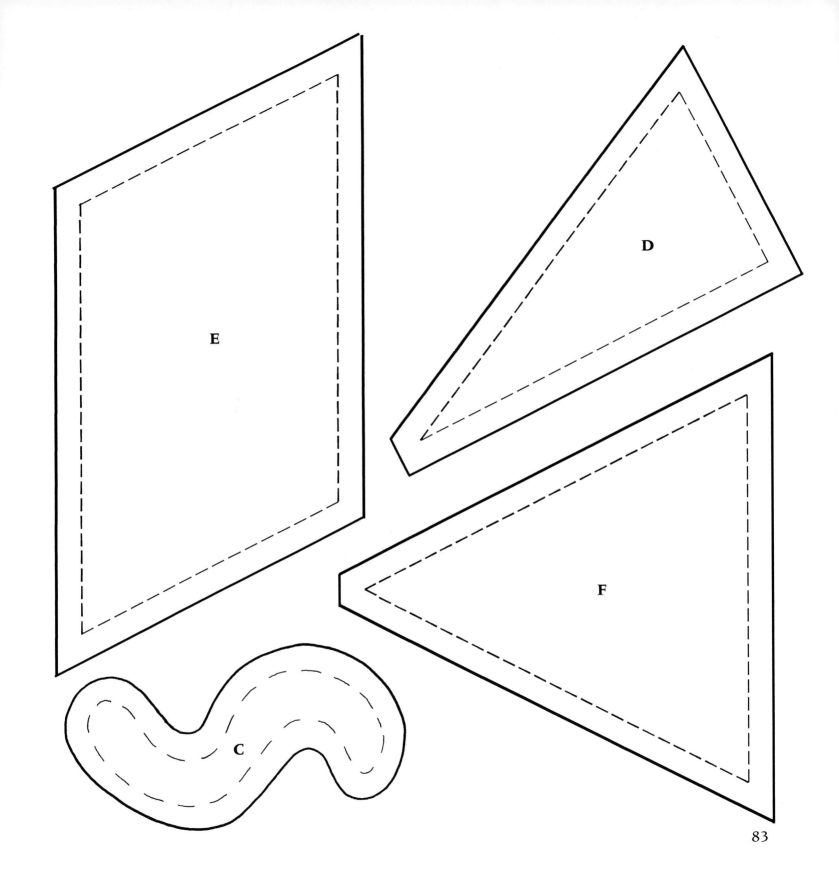

E

D

F

C

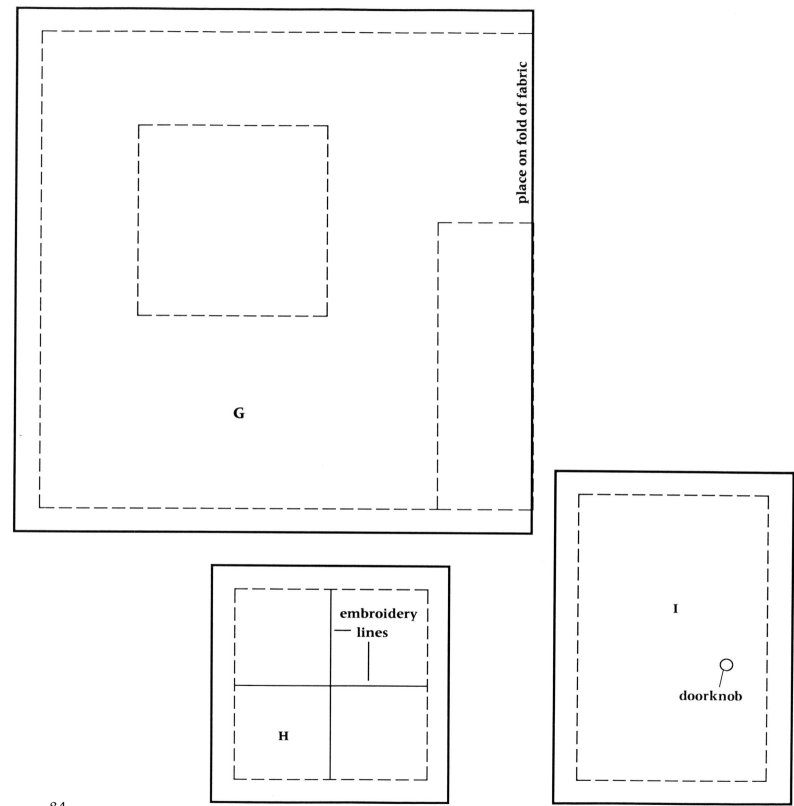

place on fold of fabric

G

embroidery
lines

H

I

doorknob

84

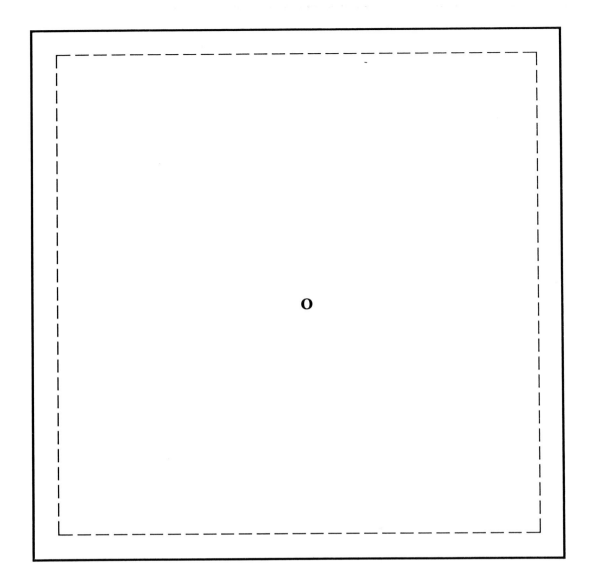

O

J

place on
fold of fabric

MINI HOME BLOCK TEMPLATES

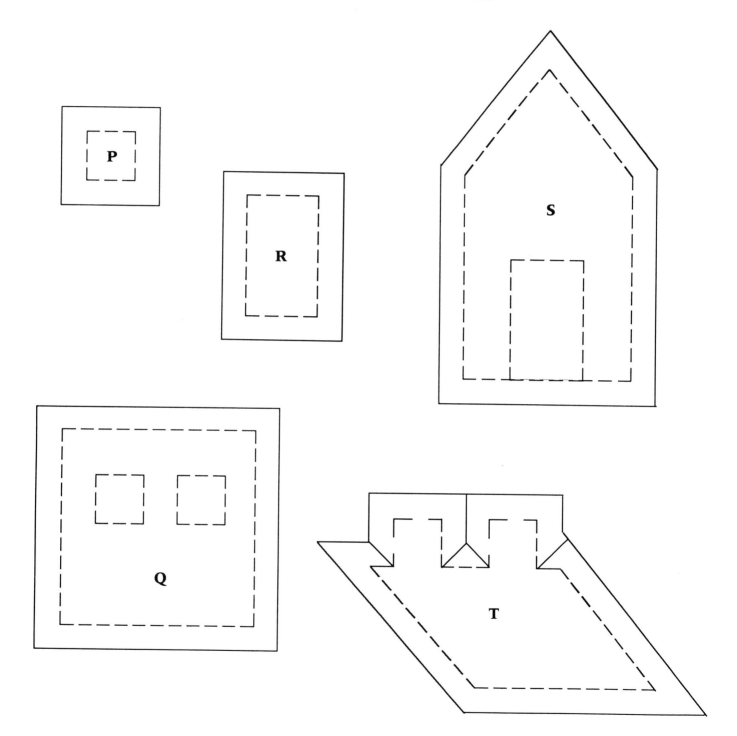

Independence Square Table Runner and Napkin Rings

This project uses the colors of the American flag to create all-American table accessories that would be perfect for a Fourth of July celebration or a cool summer supper.

The table runner is made of three red-white-and-blue Independence Square blocks surrounded by a blue border sprinkled with white star appliqués. The napkin rings—with their white and blue stars—echo the stellar motif, and a pair of red napkins completes the patriotic look.

You can further carry out the color scheme on your table by serving foods that match the accessories. There aren't many fresh foods that are true blue, but you can set out a big white bowl filled with fresh blueberries or blue grapes mixed with cherries or strawberries.

Full-size block: 9″ × 9″
Table runner: 13″ × 35″
Seam allowance: ¼″ (⅛″ for small appliqués)

SUPPLIES
(for table runner and 2 napkin rings)

Fabric:
- ½ yard white solid
- ⅛ yard medium red/white striped
  Scrap of dark red solid
- ⅛ yard light navy/white print
- 1¼ yards dark navy print
- ½ yard desired color, for backing

Belting: ⅓ yard desired color, 1″ wide

Batting: ½ yard

CUTTING GUIDE

For Independence Square Block (make 3)
- A: 8 white solid
  - 5 dark red solid
- B: 4 white solid
  - 4 medium red/white striped
  - 4 light navy/white print
- C: 8 medium red/white striped
- D: 4 white solid

Additional Pieces for Table Runner
- E (2½″-wide strip):
  - 4 dark navy print, 9½″
  - 2 dark navy print, 35½″
- Small star: 24 white solid
- Backing: 13½″ × 35½″
- Batting: 13½″ × 35½″
- Binding: 3 yards dark navy print

Additional Pieces for Napkin Ring (make 2)
    F (1¾"-wide strip):
        1 dark navy print, 6½"
    Large star:
        2 dark navy print
        1 batting
    Small star: 1 white solid*
    Belting: 6"

Seam allowance: ⅛"

DIRECTIONS

Table Runner

Make three Independence Square blocks, following step-by-step directions on page 90.

To assemble table runner front (see Table Runner Diagram): Sew together blocks and two 9½" E's, to form center of piece. Stitch remaining 9½" E's to short edges of patchwork. Stitch 35½" E's to long edges.

To appliqué (see "Appliqués" on page 13): Appliqué small stars on E border, referring to Table Runner Diagram for placement.

To quilt: Set table runner front, batting, and backing together; see "The Quilt Layers," page 15. Referring to "Quilting" (page 15), baste piece for quilting. Quilt around stars and light-colored A's, B's, and D's. Quilt the center of all E strips.

To finish: Bind table runner edges; see "Finishing the Quilt" on page 17.

Napkin Ring (make 2)

Appliqué small star (with ⅛" seam allowance) on center of one large star.

To assemble large star: Baste batting behind appliquéd large star. Baste second large star (backing) to appliquéd front, right sides together. Stitch stars together through all three layers, leaving small opening in one edge for turning. Trim seam allowance of batting close to stitching. Clip into fabric seam allowance where shown on large star pattern. Turn star to right side. Slip-stitch opening closed.
    Quilt around edges of large and small stars.

To assemble ring: Press one long edge of F ¼" to wrong side. Center belting on wrong side of F. Fold F ends smoothly over ends of belting; press. Fold long F edges over belting, overlapping raw edge along center with folded edge. Topstitch close to center fold.
    Join covered belting ends, right side out, to form ring; hand-sew ends together securely with tiny, invisible stitches.

To finish: Center appliquéd star over joining of ring ends; tack in place where indicated by X's on large star pattern.

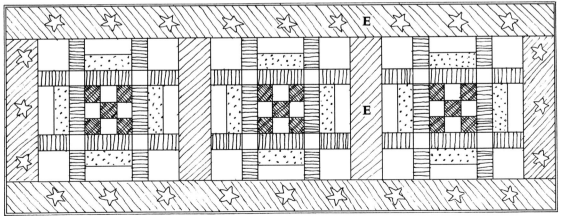

TABLE RUNNER DIAGRAM

Independence Square Block

◆◆◆◆◆◆◆◆◆◆◆◆◆◆◆◆◆◆◆

Step 1: Sew together four white and five dark A's, to form three rows.

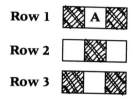

Row 1
Row 2
Row 3

Step 2: Join white/dark Rows 1–3, to complete the nine-patch.

Step 3: Sew together a white B and a light B, to form a B/B rectangle. (Make 4 B/B rectangles.)

Step 4: Stitch a medium B to a B/B rectangle, to form a B/B/B square. (Make 2 B/B/B squares.)

Step 5: Stitch pieced and plain squares and rectangles together, to form five rows.

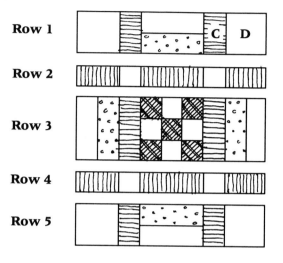

Row 1
Row 2
Row 3
Row 4
Row 5

Step 6: Join Rows 1–5, completing the block.

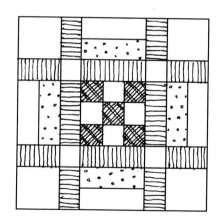

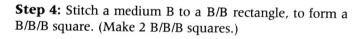

90

APPLIQUÉ PATTERNS

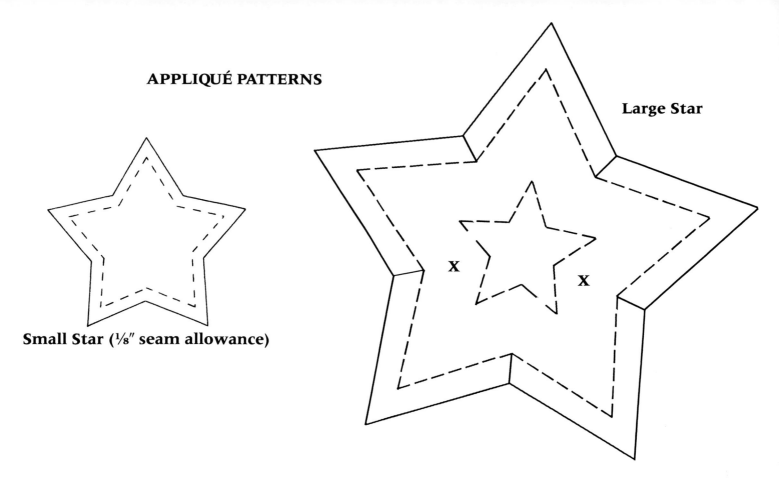

Large Star

Small Star (⅛″ seam allowance)

X   X

FULL-SIZE INDEPENDENCE SQUARE BLOCK TEMPLATES

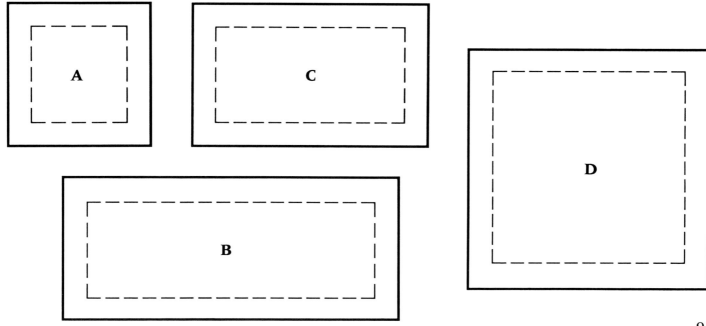

A

C

B

D

91

Jacob's Ladder Apron and Potholder

Some aprons are made to have flour-and-shortening-coated hands wiped on them as you merrily bake up a batch of cookies—but this isn't one of them. This is what I call a dress-up apron. Prepare your meal in an old, favorite apron and then, when your company arrives for that special dinner party, dazzle them by wearing this eye-catching patchwork creation.

The central design of the apron is the Jacob's Ladder mini block. The upper edge of the apron is gracefully curved and notched, and the upper edge of the pocket (which is made from one corner of the mini block) mirrors the apron's top. Bring hot dishes to the table with the coordinating potholder. Or, better yet, make and use a pair of them.

◆◆◆◆◆◆

Mini block: 6″ × 6″
Corner of mini block: 4″ × 4″
Full-size block: 12″ × 12″
Apron: Fits adult
Potholder: 8″ × 8″, plus hanging loop
Seam allowance: ¼″

◆◆◆◆◆◆

SUPPLIES
(for apron and one potholder)

Fabric:
  ⅛ yard white solid
  ⅛ yard pale peach print
  ⅛ yard light peach print
  ½ yard medium white/blue print
  2 yards dark blue print

Lightweight nonwoven interfacing: 6″ × 18″

Ribbon: 3″ peach, ½″ wide

Batting: ⅓ yard

CUTTING GUIDE

For Jacob's Ladder Block
  A: 10 pale peach print
      10 light peach print
  B: 4 white solid
      4 dark blue print

For Pocket
  A: 4 pale peach print
      4 light peach print
  B: 2 white solid
      2 dark blue print
  C (1½″-wide strip):
      2 medium white/blue print, 4½″
      1 medium white/blue print, 6½″
  Pocket top: 1 medium white/blue print
  Backing*
  Batting*

Additional Pieces for Apron

C (1½"-wide strip):
    2 medium white/blue print, 6½"
    2 medium white/blue print, 8½"
Ties (1½"-wide bias strip): 2 yards dark blue print
Apron**
Apron top***
Batting: 8" × 8"

Additional Pieces for Potholder

C (1½"-wide strip):
    2 medium white/blue print, 6½"
    2 medium white/blue print, 8½"
Backing: 8½" × 8½"
Batting: 8" × 8"

Use completed pocket front as pattern to cut one piece each from backing and batting.

**Enlarge apron pattern on 1" squares (see "Templates and Patterns" on page 21); adjust length as desired. Use enlarged pattern to cut two aprons from dark blue print (apron front and lining).*

***Use enlarged apron pattern to cut one apron top from interfacing.*

DIRECTIONS

Apron

Make one mini Jacob's Ladder block (for appliqué), following step-by-step directions on opposite page.

Make top right corner of mini block (for pocket); Make two checkered squares and two white/dark squares, following Steps 1, 2, and 4. Join pieced squares, completing block corner.

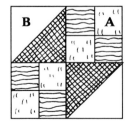

For appliqué: Stitch 6½" C's to top and bottom edges of full block; stitch 8½" C's to sides.

Pin batting, centered, to wrong side of patchwork. Referring to "The Quilt Layers" (page 15), baste piece for quilting. Quilt around white and light squares on block (see "Quilting," page 16). Quilt inner edge of C border.

Appliqué quilted block on upper section of apron, centered between apron sides (see "Appliqué" on page 13); refer to apron pattern for placement.

For pocket: Stitch 4½" C's to sides of partial block. Stitch 6½" C to bottom. Stitch pocket top to upper edge of patchwork, completing pocket front.

Stitch pocket front and backing together, right sides in, leaving 3" opening in one straight edge for turning. Clip notch on pocket top (see pocket top pattern). Turn pocket to right side. Insert batting through opening, poking it into corners with a knitting needle. Slip-stitch opening closed.

Baste and quilt pocket as for block appliqué.

Pin pocket to either left or right side of apron front; see apron pattern for placement. Machine-stitch pocket sides and bottom in place.

For ties: Cut two 14" lengths and two 18" lengths from bias strip.

To make each tie, press long edges of strip to wrong side of fabric, so that they meet along strip center. Press strip in half lengthwise along center, hiding raw edges and matching previous folds; stitch close to folds. Knot one end of each tie; trim away excess fabric close to knots.

Pin shorter ties ¼" in from ends of curved apron top with raw tie ends even with apron top and knots facing apron bottom. Pin knotted ends in place, so that ties won't get caught in stitching.

Pin longer ties ¼" down from top of straight apron sides in similar manner, so that knots face apron center. Pin knotted ends in place.

To finish: Pin lining to apron front, right sides together. Stitch side and top apron edges, leaving bottom edge open. Clip notched top as for pocket top; turn apron to right side. Remove pins.

Separate bottom edges of apron front and lining, then press ¼" to inside twice. Hand-stitch folded edges together with tiny, invisible stitches. Topstitch close to apron edges all around.

Potholder

Make one mini Jacob's Ladder block.

Stitch 6½" C's to block top and bottom. Stitch 8½" C's to sides, completing potholder front.

To assemble: Fold ribbon in half, to form 1½"-long hanging loop. Pin loop to one corner of potholder front on right side, so that ends are even with fabric edge and loop faces center.

Stitch potholder front and back together, right sides in, leaving 3" opening in one edge for turning; turn to right side. Insert batting. Slip-stitch opening closed.

To finish: Baste and quilt potholder as for appliquéd block on apron.

Jacob's Ladder Block
◆◆◆◆◆◆◆◆◆◆◆◆◆◆◆◆

Step 1: Sew together a pale A and a light A, to form a rectangle. (Make 2 white/light rectangles.)

Step 2: Sew pieces from Step 1 together, to form a checkered square.

Step 3: Make four more checkered squares, following Steps 1 and 2.

Step 4: Sew together a white B and a dark B, to form a white/dark square.

Step 5: Make three more white/dark squares, following Step 4.

Step 6: Stitch pieced squares together, to form three rows.

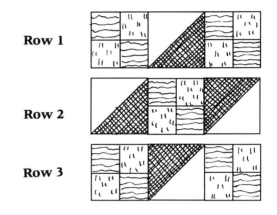

Row 1

Row 2

Row 3

Step 7: Join Rows 1–3, completing the block.

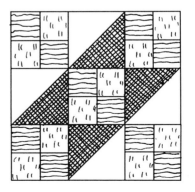

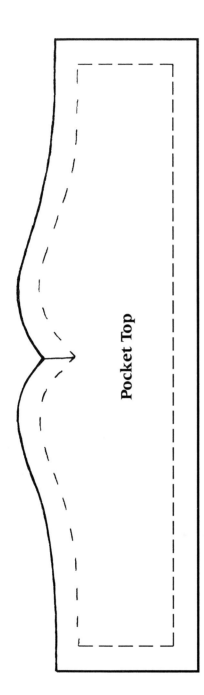

Pocket Top

APRON PATTERN

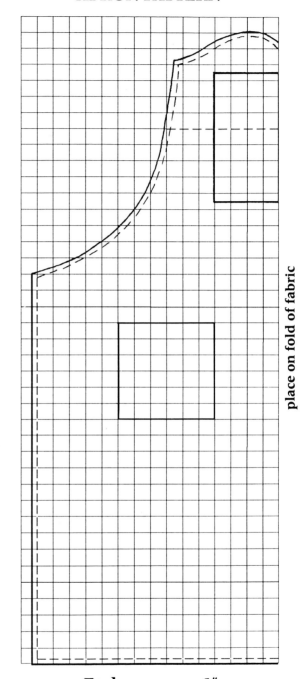

place on fold of fabric

Each square = 1″

FULL-SIZE JACOB'S LADDER BLOCK TEMPLATES

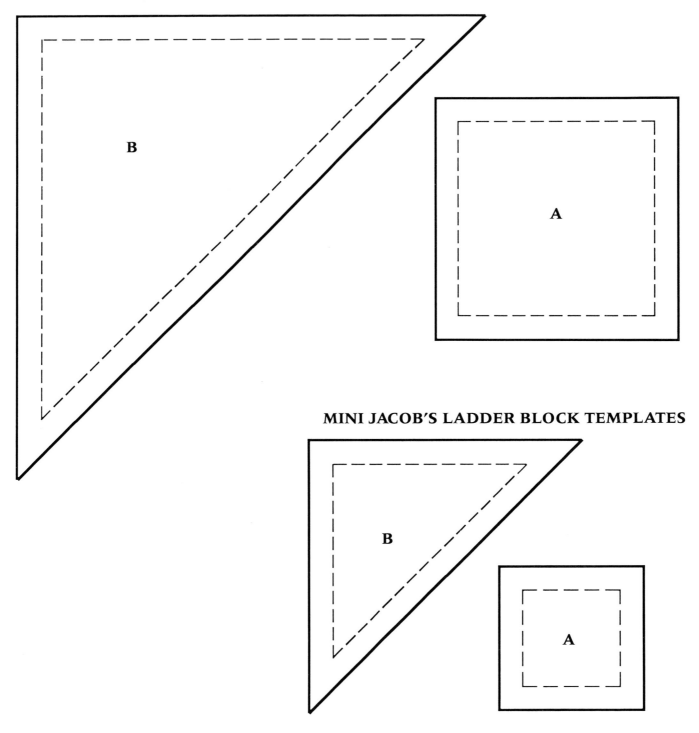

B

A

MINI JACOB'S LADDER BLOCK TEMPLATES

B

A

Kansas Trouble Quilt

The first quilting class I ever took was held in the large, hacienda-style house of my teacher in San Diego. She always had so many quilts stacked around her home that I wondered what she kept on her bed. One day I finally asked, and her answer really surprised me: She said whichever quilt she was working on was what she used at night. Her quilt-in-progress went right on her bed—needle, hoop, and all!

I learned a lot from that teacher, but I never use my in-progress quilts the way she did. I designed this project in my favorite colors so that I could enjoy it on my bed—after it was completed!—although now and then I switch quilts, for the sake of variety. (My favorite alternate is an antique, appliquéd Flower Ring quilt that was made in the 1920s.)

The Kansas Trouble pattern reminds me of the tornados that Kansas is famous for. I love the feeling of energy and movement in the main body of the quilt. To provide tranquility for balance, I added a graceful, appliquéd vine border.

◆◆◆◆◆◆

Full-size blocks: 16″ × 16″
Quilt: 75½″ × 75½″
Seam allowance: ¼″

◆◆◆◆◆◆

SUPPLIES

Fabric:
    3 yards white solid
    1 yard medium green solid
    ¾ yard light purple solid
    2 yards medium purple/green/peach print
    1¾ yards medium-dark purple solid
    ½ yard dark purple solid
    5 yards desired color, for backing

Batting: 4½ yards

CUTTING GUIDE

For Dark Kansas Trouble Block (make 8)
    A: 4 white solid
        4 medium purple/green/peach print
    B: 24 white solid
       24 dark purple solid
    C: 4 white solid

For Light Kansas Trouble Block (make 8)
    A: 4 white solid
        4 medium purple/green/peach print
    B: 24 white solid
       24 light purple solid
    C: 4 white solid

Additional Pieces
    D (1¾″-wide strip):
        2 medium-dark purple solid, 64½″
        2 medium-dark purple solid, 67″
        2 medium-dark purple solid, 73″
        2 medium-dark purple solid 75½″

E (3½"-wide strip):
    2 white solid, 67"
    2 white solid, 73"
F (⅝"-wide bias strip): 8½ yards medium green
    solid
Leaf: 68 medium green solid
Bud: 4 medium green solid
Bud tip: 4 light purple solid
Backing: 79½" × 79½"
Batting: 75½" × 75½"
Binding: 8½ yards medium-dark purple solid

DIRECTIONS

Make eight full-size dark Kansas Trouble blocks, following step-by-step directions on opposite page. Make eight full-size light Kansas Trouble blocks, substituting light purple B's for dark B's.

To assemble quilt front (see Quilt Diagram): Stitch blocks together, to form four rows with four blocks in each row.

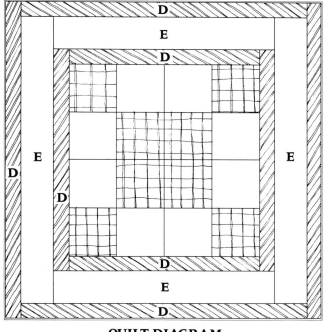

QUILT DIAGRAM

100

For inner border, stitch 64½" D's to top and bottom edges of patchwork; stitch 67" D's to sides.

For middle border, stitch shorter E's to top and bottom edges of piece; stitch longer E's to sides.

For outer border, stitch 73" D's to patchwork top and bottom; stitch 75½" D's to sides.

To appliqué (see "Appliqué," page 13): To make vine, fold green strip in half lengthwise, right side out; stitch ⅛" from long raw edges; trim seam allowance to 1/16". Flatten and press strip, hiding stitching and seam allowance underneath.

Arrange and pin vine on E border; cut vine ends in corners, so that fabric lies flat and smooth. Appliqué vine in place.

Appliqué a bud, bud tip, and pair of leaves on each corner, covering cut vine ends. Appliqué remainder of leaves along vine as shown.

To quilt: Transfer quilting motif to white A's; see "The Quilt Layers" on page 14.

Set quilt front, batting, and backing together. Referring to "Quilting" (page 15), baste piece for quilting. Quilt bud-and-leaves motif. Quilt around main applique and outlines.

To finish: Trim backing even with quilt front and batting. Bind quilt edges; see "Finishing the Quilt" on page 18.

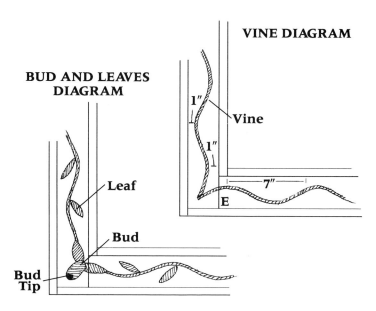

BUD AND LEAVES DIAGRAM

VINE DIAGRAM

Kansas Trouble Block

Step 1: Sew together a white A and a medium A, to form a square.

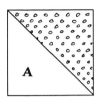

Step 2: Sew together a white B and a dark B, to form a square. (Make 6 B/B squares.)

Step 3: Stitch three B/B squares together.

Step 4: Stitch piece from Step 3 to piece from Step 1.

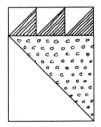

Step 5: Stitch three B/B squares and a white C together.

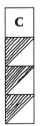

Step 6: Join pieces from Steps 4 and 5, to complete the quarter-block.

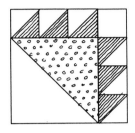

Step 7: Make three more quarter-blocks, following Steps 1–6.

Step 8: Join the four quarter-blocks, completing the block.

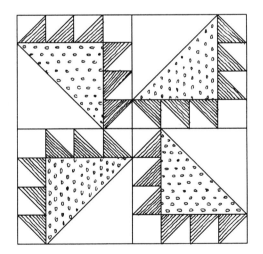

APPLIQUÉ PATTERNS

Leaf

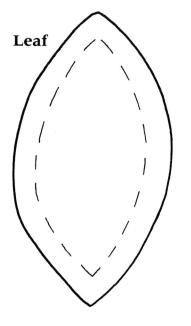

Bud

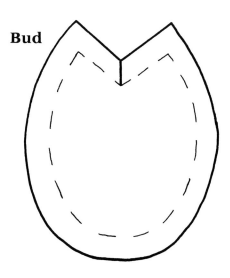

Bud Tip

QUILTING MOTIF

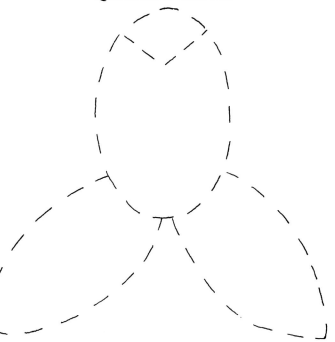

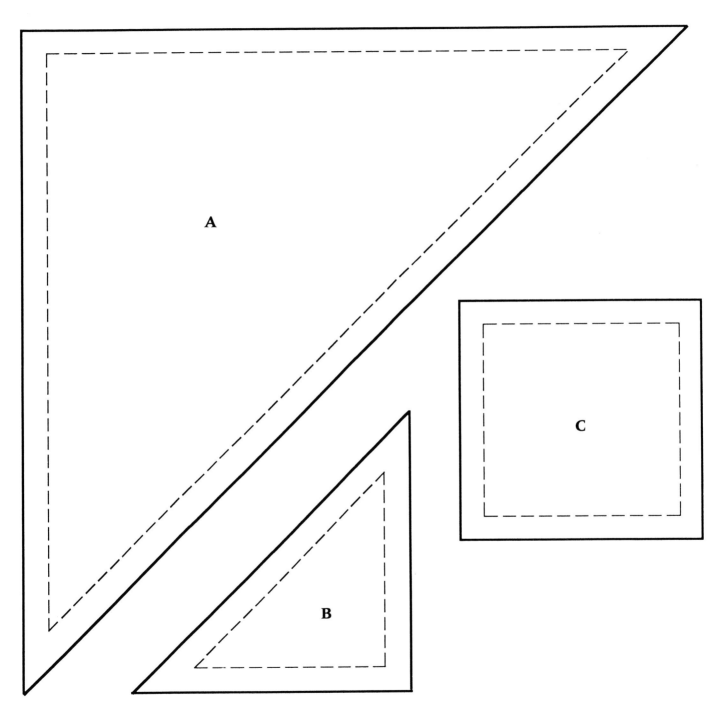

A

B

C

Louisiana Wallhanging and Pillow

Looking at the photograph of the Louisiana Wallhanging and Pillow reminds me how warm and cozy it feels to sit in my rocker with a cup of hot cocoa, listening to beautiful music and watching the flames flicker and dance in the fireplace.

I had always wanted to have a fireplace in my bedroom, and when I remodeled the upstairs of my home, I finally got my wish. I looked for a mantel that would be appropriate in my turn-of-the-century house for many months. At last I found this antique, which was built in the same year as my house, 1904.

Decorating the mantel is the project's wall-hanging, which is made of 5" × 5" mini blocks: two Louisiana blocks, a Tulip block, and three letter blocks (you can use your initials). Complementing the wallhanging is a pillow made from a full-size 10" × 10" Louisiana block.

◆◆◆◆◆◆

Mini Louisiana block: **5" × 5"**
Full-size Louisiana block: **10" × 10"**
Mini Tulip block: **5" × 5"**
Mini letter blocks: **5" × 5"**
Wallhanging: **21½" × 15½"**
Pillow: **14" × 14", plus piping**
Seam allowance: **¼"**

◆◆◆◆◆◆

SUPPLIES

(for wallhanging and one pillow)

Fabric:
- ⅓ yard white solid
- ¼ yard light rust print
- ⅛ yard dark rust print
    Scrap of dark rust solid
- ⅛ yard medium green solid
- ⅛ yard light green print
- ¼ yard medium green print
- ¼ yard dark green print #1
- ¾ yard dark green print #2
- ½ yard desired color, for backing

Piping: 1⅔ yards red, for pillow

Batting: ½ yard

Fiberfill, for stuffing pillow

Plastic rings, for hanging quilt

CUTTING GUIDE

For Mini Louisiana Block (make 2)
- A: 8 medium green solid
- B: 4 dark rust print
- C: 4 white solid

For Full-Size Louisana Block
- A: 8 light green print
- B: 4 dark rust print
- C: 4 white solid

For Mini Tulip Block

D: 2 white solid (1 reversed)
   2 medium green solid (1 reversed)
E: 4 white solid
   4 light rust print
   4 medium green solid
F: 3 white solid
   3 light rust print
   2 dark rust solid
G: 2 medium green solid
H: 3 light rust print

For Letter Blocks

Refer to Patchwork Alphabet Quilt (page 199). Follow Cutting Guide for three letter blocks: Cut all white solid pieces as directed. Cut nonwhite pieces for center block from medium green print. Cut nonwhite pieces for side blocks from light rust print.

Additional Pieces for Wallhanging

I (1½"-wide strip):
   2 white solid, 5½"
   2 medium green print, 15½"
   2 medium green print, 19½"
   2 dark green print #1, 5½"
   2 dark green print #1, 13½"
   3 dark green print #1, 17½"
Backing: 25½" × 19½"
Batting: 21½" × 15½"
Binding: 2¼ yards dark green print #2

Additional Pieces for Pillow

J (2½"-wide strip):
   2 dark green print #2, 10½"
   2 dark green print #2, 14½"
Backing: 14½" × 14½"
Batting: 14½" × 14½"

DIRECTIONS

Wallhanging

Make two mini Louisiana blocks, following step-by-step directions on page 108.

Make three mini letter blocks; see Patchwork Alphabet Quilt.

Make one mini Tulip block as follows.

Step 1: Sew together a white D and a medium D, to form a rectangle.

Step 2: Make another D/D rectangle, using reversed D's.

Step 3: Sew together a white E and a medium E, to form a square. (Make 2 white/medium squares.)

Step 4: Sew together a white E and a light E. (Make 2 white/light squares.)

Step 5: Sew together a light E and a medium E. (Make 2 light/medium squares.)

Step 6: Stitch three white F's and a dark F together.

Step 7: Stitch three light F's and a dark F together.

Step 8: Stitch pieced and plain rectangles and squares together, to form five rows.

| Row 1 | Row 2 | Row 3 | Row 4 | Row 5 |

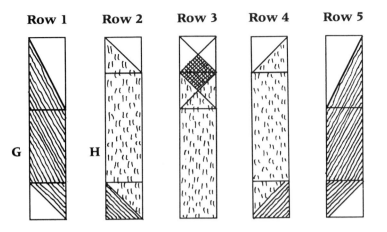

Step 9: Join Rows 1–5, completing the block.

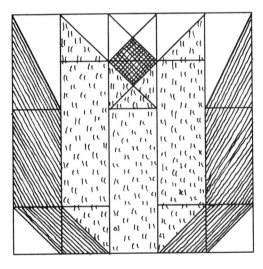

To assemble quilt front (see Quilt Diagram): Sew together Louisiana blocks, Tulip block, and two dark green 5½" I's, to form top row of quilt.

For bottom row, stitch letter blocks together; stitch white 5½" I's to side blocks.

For inner borders, stitch 17½" I's to top and bottom of top row of patchwork. Stitch remaining 17½" I to bottom of bottom row of patchwork. Stitch 13½" I's to sides.

For outer border, stitch 19½" I's to patchwork top and bottom; stitch 15½" I's to sides.

To quilt: Set quilt front, batting, and backing together (see "The Quilt Layers," page 14). Referring to "Quilting" (page 15), baste piece for quilting. Quilt around initials, Louisiana blocks, Tulip blocks, and I strips.

To finish: Trim backing even with quilt front and batting. Bind quilt edges; see "Finishing the Quilt" on page 17. Attach rings for hanging.

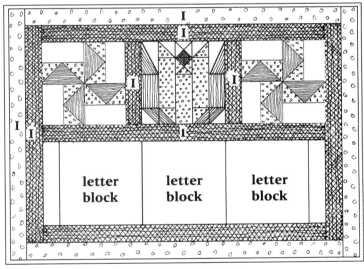

QUILT DIAGRAM

107

Pillow

Make a full-size Louisiana block, substituting light green A's for medium A's.

To quilt: Mark quilting lines on C's. Baste batting to wrong side of pillow front. Quilt C's on marked lines.

To assemble pillow: Prepare piping ends; see "Finishing the Quilt" on page 17. Baste piping all around pillow front on right side, matching raw edges.
   Stitch backing to pillow front, right sides together, leaving 3" opening in one edge for turning; turn to right side. Stuff pillow firmly with fiberfill, poking it into corners with a knitting needle. Slip-stitch opening closed.

seam lines   **outer edges of patchwork**

quilting lines
C

PILLOW QUILTING DIAGRAM

Louisiana Block

Step 1: Stitch two medium A's to a dark B.

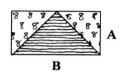

Step 2: Join a white C and piece from Step 1, to complete the quarter-block.

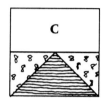

Step 3: Make three more quarter-blocks, following Steps 1 and 2.

Step 4: Join the four quarter-blocks, completing the block.

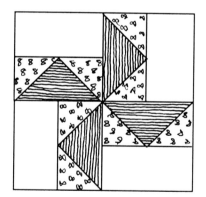

FULL-SIZE LOUISIANA BLOCK TEMPLATES

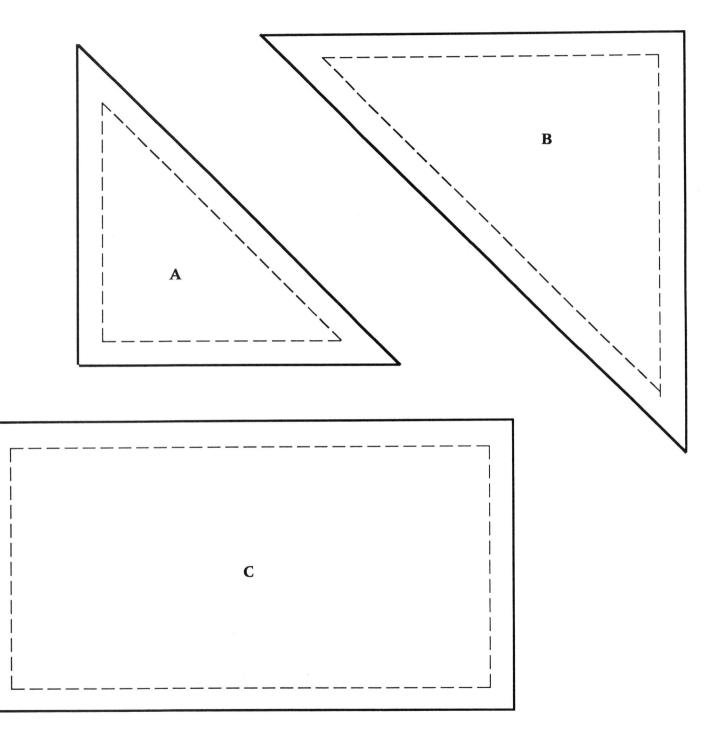

MINI LOUISIANA BLOCK TEMPLATES

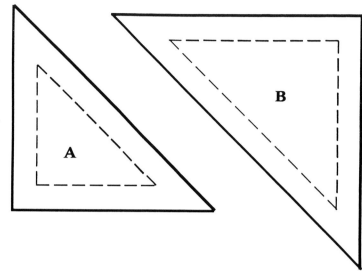

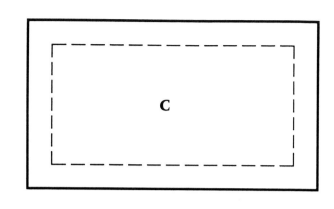

MINI TULIP BLOCK TEMPLATES

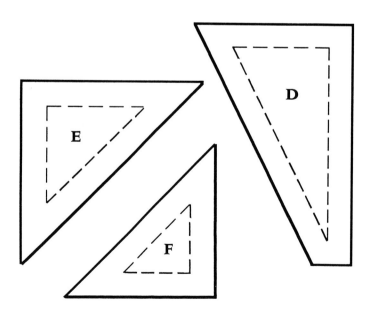

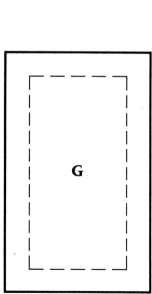

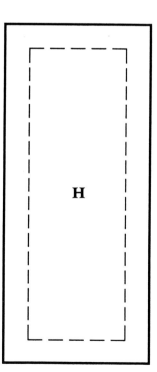

Mosaic Basket Cover

My inspiration for the Mosaic Basket Cover came from the show *Oklahoma*, a production of which I saw not long ago in San Diego. In one scene of the show, a "box social" was held: The women of the town made scrumptious lunches and packed them in decorative baskets, which were then auctioned off to the town's menfolk. The highest bidder on each basket also won the privilege of eating his lunch with the creative woman who had made it.

I imagined a romantic picnic lunch packed in a basket that was covered with patchwork and embellished with hearts. I live near the sea, so I pictured a lunch for two on a blanket or quilt spread out on the sand by the water's edge.

If the basket cover gets a little smudged during use, don't fret—it can be cleaned in a washing machine and will come out looking as good as new.

Mini block: 6" × 6"
Full-size block: 12" × 12"
Basket cover: 19" × 12", plus lace edging
Seam allowance: ¼"

SUPPLIES
(for basket cover and 2 fasteners)

Fabric:
  ¼ yard white solid
  ½ yard light pink print
  ¼ yard medium blue print
  ⅓ yard dark blue print

Ribbon: 1⅓ yards dark blue, ½" wide

Cotton eyelet lace: 2 yards white, 2¼" wide

Batting: ½ yard

Snap fasteners: 4 small

Wicker basket: 17" × 10", with 1"-wide handle

White spray paint

CUTTING GUIDE

For Mosaic Block (make 2)
  A: 16 white solid
  B: 4 light pink print
     4 medium blue print

Additional Pieces for Basket Cover
  C (2½"-wide strip):
     2 dark blue print, 6½"
     4 dark blue print, 8½"
  D (1½"-wide strip):
     2 light pink print, 12½"
     2 light pink print, 17½"
     1 dark blue print, 10½"
  Lace: 2 lengths, 32"
  Backing: 19½" × 12½" white solid
  Batting: 19" × 12"

Additional Pieces for Heart Fastener (make 2)

E: 2 white solid
   1 light pink print
   1 medium blue print
Heart:
   1 front*
   1 backing, white solid
   1 batting (minus seam allowance)
Ribbon: 2 lengths, 12"

See Directions for cutting heart front.

DIRECTIONS

Prepare basket by spraying with two coats white paint; allow paint to dry thoroughly after each coat.

Make basket cover and two fasteners as follows, then attach to basket: Place cover on basket and snap on fasteners, securing lace around basket handle.

Basket Cover

Make two mini Mosaic blocks (one Block I and one Block II), following step-by-step directions on page 114.

To make cover top: Stitch a blue 6½″ C to one side of each block; see Cover Diagram for placement. Stitch 8½″ C's to top and bottom edges of each block. Stitch together blocks and blue 10½″ D as shown. Stitch longer pink D's to patchwork top and bottom; stitch shorter pink D's to sides.

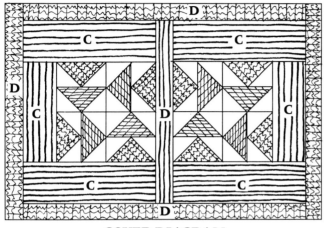

COVER DIAGRAM

To attach lace: Press lace ends ½″ to wrong side. Baste lace to each half of cover top (see Lace Diagram for placement) on right side of fabric, matching raw (outer) edges.

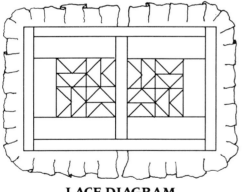

LACE DIAGRAM

To assemble: Baste batting to wrong side of cover top, centered. Stitch backing to cover top, right sides together, leaving 3″ opening in one side for turning; turn to right side; lace will extend beyond cover. Slip-stitch opening closed.

To quilt: Referring to "Quilting" (page 15), baste piece for quilting. Outline quilt C and D strips and around white A triangles in Mosaic blocks.

To finish: Sew snap halves to lace ends, ¼″ from folds (see Snaps Placement Diagram).

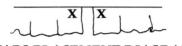

SNAPS PLACEMENT DIAGRAM

Heart Fastener (make 2)

Stitch E's together, to form a checkered square; see Fastener Diagram. Cut heart shape from checkered square.

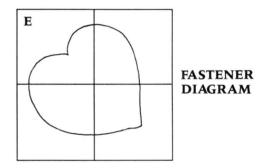

FASTENER DIAGRAM

To assemble: Baste batting heart to wrong side of heart front, centered. Stitch backing to heart front, right sides together, leaving a small opening for turning; clip into seam allowance along curves. Turn heart to right side.

To quilt: Quilt around white E's and outer edges of heart.

To finish: Fold two ribbon lengths in half; stitch to back of heart (see Ribbon Diagram). Sew snap halves to ribbons.

RIBBON DIAGRAM

Mosaic Block

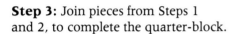

Block I

Step 1: Stitch two A's to a light B, to form a rectangle.

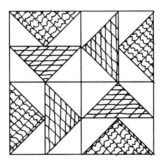

Step 2: Stitch two A's to a medium B.

Step 3: Join pieces from Steps 1 and 2, to complete the quarter-block.

Step 4: Make three more quarter-blocks, following Steps 1–3.

Step 5: Join the four quarter-blocks, completing the block.

Block II

Step 1: Make four quarter-blocks, following Steps 1–3 of Block I.

Step 2: Join the four quarter-blocks, completing the block.

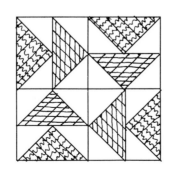

114

HEART FASTENER TEMPLATES

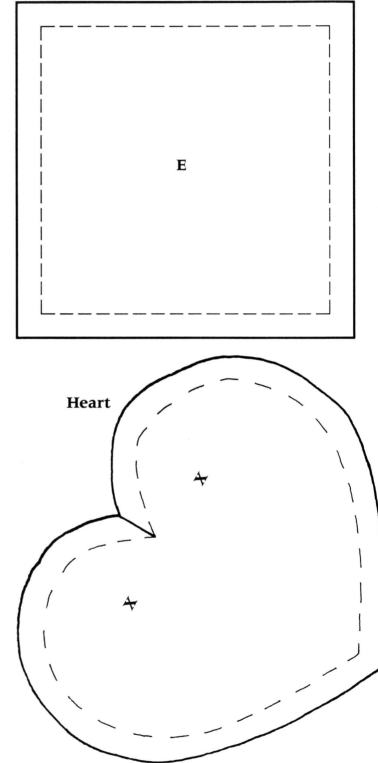

E

Heart

FULL-SIZE MOSAIC BLOCK TEMPLATES

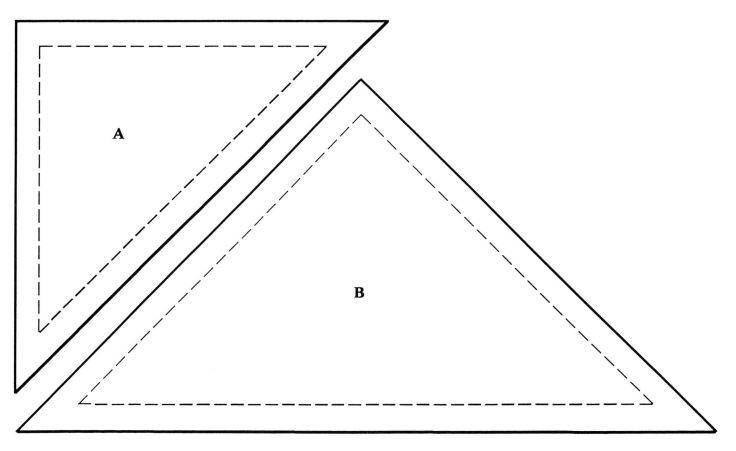

MINI MOSAIC BLOCK TEMPLATES

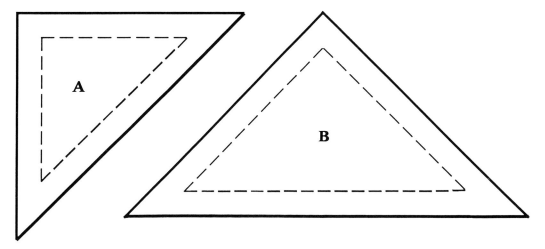

115

Next-Door Neighbor Tote Bag

During my early days of designing, I loved to enter the Home Arts division of the annual Southern California Expo. I can still remember how proud I was of the prize ribbons that were awarded to me for sewing, dollmaking, and embroidery. I saved my ribbons and even though they are now old and wrinkled, they are still cherished mementos of personal accomplishments—and they were my inspiration for this tote bag.

I actually designed this project over ten years ago. I never got around to making the patterns or sample then, but I saved the idea in my "To Do" folder. While I was compiling material for this book, I went through my folder and the sketch of the tote bag caught my eye.

This project is a challenging one: The techniques include patchwork, appliqué, embroidery, and quilting. The finished tote bag can be used to hold your latest quilting endeavor, or it can be hung on the wall as an "I'm hooked on quilting" decoration.

Mini block: 4″ × 4″
Full-size block: 8″ × 8″
Tote bag: 16″ × 16″, plus handles
Seam allowance: ¼″

SUPPLIES

Fabric:
- ⅛ yard white solid
- ⅓ yard light white/pink print
- ½ yard light pink print
- ⅛ yard medium pink print
- ⅛ yard dark pink print
- ⅛ yard pale green print
  Scrap of medium green/white striped
- ½ yard dark green solid

Batting: ½ yard

Cotton eyelet lace: ½ yard white, ½″ wide

Piping: 1 yard white

Embroidery floss: 1 skein dark pink

CUTTING GUIDE

For Next-Door Neighbor Block (make 4)
- A: 4 medium pink print
  - 8 dark pink print
  - 12 pale green print
- B: 4 pale green print

Additional Pieces
- C (4½″ × 8½″):
  - 1 light white/pink print
- D (2½″-wide strip):
  - 2 white solid, 12½″
  - 2 light pink print, 12½″
  - 2 light pink print, 16½″

E (16½″ × 16½″):
    1 light pink print
    2 dark green solid
F (3½″-wide strip): 2 light pink print, 14½″
Circle: 1 medium green/white striped
Left ribbon: 1 dark pink print
Right ribbon: 1 dark pink print
Heart: 2 medium pink print
Batting:
    Two 16″ × 16″
    Two 1½″ × 14½″

TOTE BAG DIAGRAM

DIRECTIONS

Make four mini Next-Door Neighbor blocks, following step-by-step directions on opposite page.

To embroider: Transfer "1st PRIZE" to fabric circle (see "The Quilt Layers," page 14). Transfer "QUILTING WON" to one white D. Transfer "MY HEART" to second white D.

Embroider "1st" in backstitch. Embroider remaining words in chain stitch.

To appliqué (see "Appliqué," page 13): Press one end of lace ¼″ to wrong side. Beginning with folded end, baste lace to embroidered circle, right sides together, with raw edges even; overlap ends. Stitch lace in place. Press edges of circle and lace ¼″ to wrong side, hiding raw edges and stitching line; lace will extend beyond fabric edge.

Appliqué left ribbon, right ribbon, and circle on C; see Tote Bag Diagram for placement.

Appliqué hearts on "MY HEART" D strip.

To make bag front: Stitch Next-Door Neighbor blocks together in pairs. Stitch pairs of blocks to C. Stitch embroidered D's to top and bottom edges of patchwork.

For border, stitch 12½″ pink D's to top and bottom of piece; stitch 16½″ pink D's to sides.

To quilt: Pin one square batting piece to wrong side of bag front, centered. Referring to "Quilting" (page 15), baste piece for quilting. Quilt around patchwork blocks, C, and embroidered D's.

To assemble bag: Baste second square batting piece to wrong side of pink E (bag back), centered. Pin bag back to bag front, right sides together; stitch side and bottom edges, leaving top edge open. Turn bag to right side.

Prepare piping ends; see "Finishing the Quilt" on page 17. Baste piping all around bag top on right side of fabric, matching raw (outer) edges.

Sew together green E's (lining front and back) as for bag front and back; do not turn to right side. Separate top lining edges and press ¼″ to outside.

To make handles (make 2): For each handle, press one long edge of an F ¼″ to wrong side. Center one batting strip on wrong side of F. Fold long F edges over batting, overlapping raw edges along center; pin. Topstitch close to center fold.

Pin one handle to bag front, so that ends are even with top edge of bag front and handles face bottom. Machine-stitch handle ends in place ¼″ from fabric edge.

Attach second handle to bag back in same manner.

To finish: Press top edges of bag front and back ¼″ to inside; handles will extend above bag. Insert lining into bag, matching seams and folds. Hand-sew lining top to bag top with tiny, invisible stitches.

118

Next-Door Neighbor Block

◆◆◆◆◆◆◆◆◆◆◆◆◆◆◆◆◆◆

Step 1: Sew together a pale A and a dark A, to form a square. (Make 2 pale/dark squares.)

Step 2: Stitch pieces from Step 1 together.

Step 3: Sew together a pale A and a medium A, to form a square.

Step 4: Stitch a B and piece from Step 3 together.

Step 5: Join pieces from Steps 2 and 4, to complete the quarter-block.

Step 6: Make three more quarter blocks, following Steps 1–5.

Step 7: Join the four quarter-blocks, completing the block.

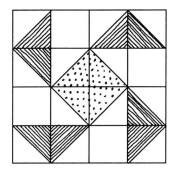

APPLIQUÉ PATTERNS

1st PRIZE

Heart

119

Left Ribbon

center

center

120

Right Ribbon

center

NG WON

center

EART ♥

121

FULL-SIZE NEXT-DOOR NEIGHBOR BLOCK TEMPLATES

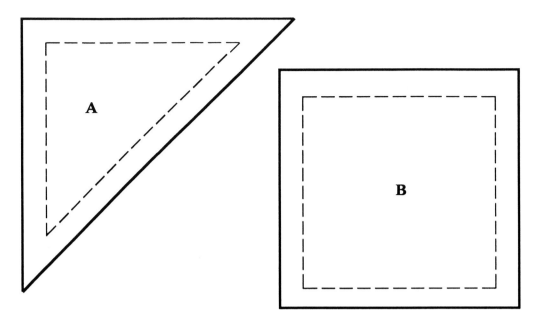

MINI NEXT-DOOR NEIGHBOR BLOCK TEMPLATES

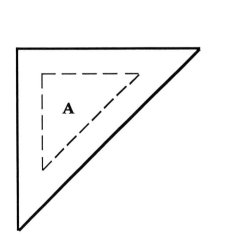

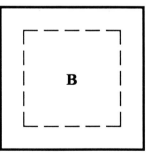

Ohio Star Tea Cozy and Napkins

I've always liked miniature patchwork because its diminutive size makes it appear much more complicated to create than it actually is. I also think it's fun to embellish purchased or premade items—so the design for this project was a natural for me.

The tea cozy is a plain white purchased one with three mini blocks set above the embroidered "HOT TEA" appliqué. A single mini block adorns one corner of the napkin. Even though you can also decorate purchased napkins, a set of four handmade ones takes almost no time at all to cut out and hem.

I think that the miniature appliqués give these simple items a finished, elegant look. I hope you agree and that you enjoy making and using them as much as I have.

◆◆◆◆◆◆

Mini block: 3″ × 3″
Full-size block: 9″ × 9″
Tea cozy: 14″ × 12″
Napkin: 16″ × 16″
Seam allowance: ¼″

◆◆◆◆◆◆

SUPPLIES

(for tea cozy and 4 napkins)

Fabric:
- ¼ yard white solid
- 1 yard medium green solid (to make 4 napkins)
- ⅛ yard light purple print
- ⅛ yard dark purple print

Embroidery floss:
- 1 skein medium green
- 1 skein dark purple

Purchased white tea cozy: 14″ × 12″

CUTTING GUIDE

For Ohio Star Block (make 7)
- A: 8 light purple print
  8 dark purple print
- B: 4 white solid
  1 dark purple print

Additional Pieces
- C: 1 white solid (for tea cozy)
- D: 4 medium green solid, 17″ × 17″ (for 4 napkins)

DIRECTIONS

Make seven mini Ohio Star blocks, following step-by-step directions on opposite page.

Tea Cozy

Sew three blocks together, to form a strip. Appliqué pieced strip on tea cozy front, about 5″ up from bottom (see "Appliqué," page 13).

Transfer embroidery pattern for "HOT TEA," vines, and leaves to C (see "The Quilt Layers," page 14), centering design. Work satin stitch to fill letters with purple floss and leaves with green. Use green to backstitch vines.

Appliqué embroidered C on tea cozy front, about ½″ below patchwork.

Napkins (set of 4)

Press edges of D's ¼″ to wrong side twice; topstitch close to inner folds.

Appliqué a block on one corner of each napkin.

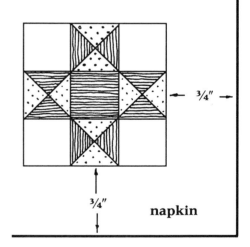

¾″

¾″

napkin

Ohio Star Block

◆◆◆◆◆◆◆◆◆◆◆◆

Step 1: Sew together a light A and a dark A, to form a triangle. (Make 8 A/A triangles.)

Step 2: Sew together two A/A triangles, to form a square. (Make 4 squares.)

Step 3: Stitch pieced and plain squares together, to form three rows.

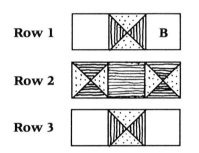

Row 1   B

Row 2

Row 3

Step 4: Join Rows, 1–3, completing the block.

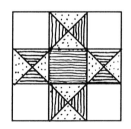

EMBROIDERY PATTERN

HOT TEA

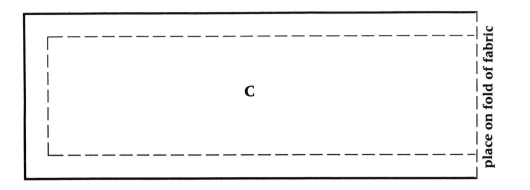

place on fold of fabric

C

FULL-SIZE OHIO STAR BLOCK TEMPLATES

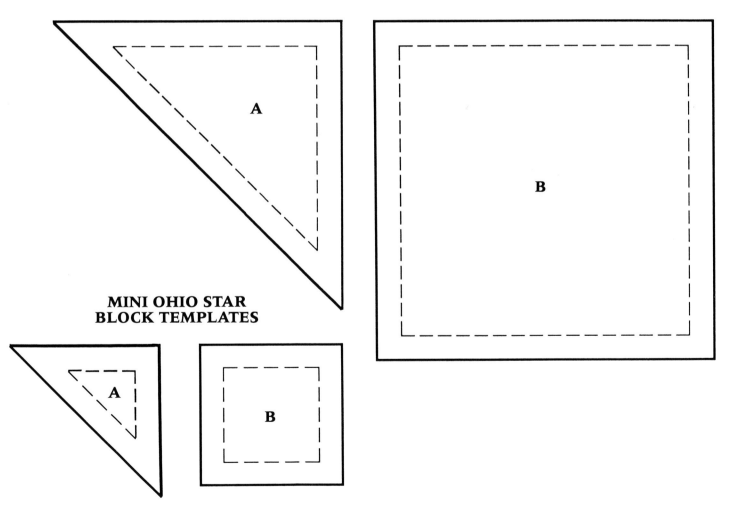

A

B

MINI OHIO STAR BLOCK TEMPLATES

A

B

126

Prairie Queen Quilt

I often like to get away by myself, to work on my books or to develop new design ideas. One of my favorite places to stay is a bed-and-breakfast called the Saratoga Inn—a wonderful old house on Whidbey Island, a short ferry ride from my home. Its walls are decorated with quilts, and the inn has an extensive library of creative books, which makes it a real "home away from home" for me.

During one of my stays there, I came across a dictionary of quilt patterns, a book that I hadn't seen before. One of the designs in it that I particularly liked was the Prairie Queen pattern, which I sketched in my design notebook and put out of my mind. While gathering ideas for *A Patchwork Alphabet*, I found the pattern in my notebook and knew it was perfect for the "P" project.

I made the Prairie Queen Quilt to fit a single bed and gave the sample to my niece, Jenni, for her sixteenth birthday. Jenni loves peach as much as I do, and the quilt coordinates well with the colors in her bedroom. She was delighted with her gift and has started her own quilt collection.

Full-size block: 9″ × 9″
Border block: 3″ × 3″
Quilt: 57½″ × 75½″
Seam allowance: ¼″

SUPPLIES

Fabric:
  3¾ yards white solid
   3 yards light peach print
   3 yards medium peach print
   2 yards dark peach print
   5 yards desired color, for backing

Batting: 2¼ yards

CUTTING GUIDE

For Prairie Queen Block (make 35)
  A: 8 light peach print
      8 dark peach print
  B: 16 white solid
  C: 4 white solid
      4 medium peach print
  D: 1 white solid

For Border Block (make 84)
  A: 2 medium peach print
      2 dark peach print
  B: 4 white solid

Additional Pieces

E (3½"-wide strip):
  2 dark peach print, 45½"
  2 dark peach print, 69½"
Backing: 61½" × 79½"
Batting: 57½" × 75½"
Binding: 4 yards medium peach print

DIRECTIONS

Make 35 full-size Prairie Queen blocks, following step-by-step directions on opposite page.

Make 84 diamond-in-a-square border blocks, following Steps 1–3 and substituting medium A's for light A's.

To assemble quilt front (see photograph): Stitch Prairie Queen blocks together, to form seven rows with five blocks in each row. Join rows, completing quilt center.

For plain border, stitch 45½" E's to top and bottom edges of patchwork; stitch 69½" E's to sides.

For pieced border, sew together border blocks to form two 17-block strips and two 25-block strips. Stitch shorter pieced strips to patchwork top and bottom; stitch longer pieced strips to sides.

To quilt: Set quilt front, batting, and backing together (see ''The Quilt Layers,'' page 14). Referring to ''Quilting'' (page 15), baste piece for quilting. Quilt around all B's, C's, D's, and E strips.

To finish: Trim backing even with quilt front and batting. Bind quilt edges; see ''Finishing the Quilt'' on page 17.

Prairie Queen Block

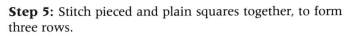

Step 1: Sew together a light A and a dark A, to form a rectangle. (Make 8 rectangles.)

Step 2: Stitch two rectangles together, to form a square. (Make 4 light/dark squares.)

Step 3: Stitch four B's to a light/dark square, to form a diamond-in-a-square. (Make 4 diamonds-in-squares.)

Step 4: Sew together a white C and a medium C, to form a square. (Make 4 squares.)

Step 5: Stitch pieced and plain squares together, to form three rows.

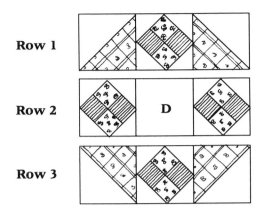

Row 1

Row 2

Row 3

Step 6: Join Rows 1–3, completing the block.

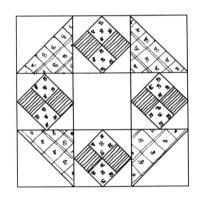

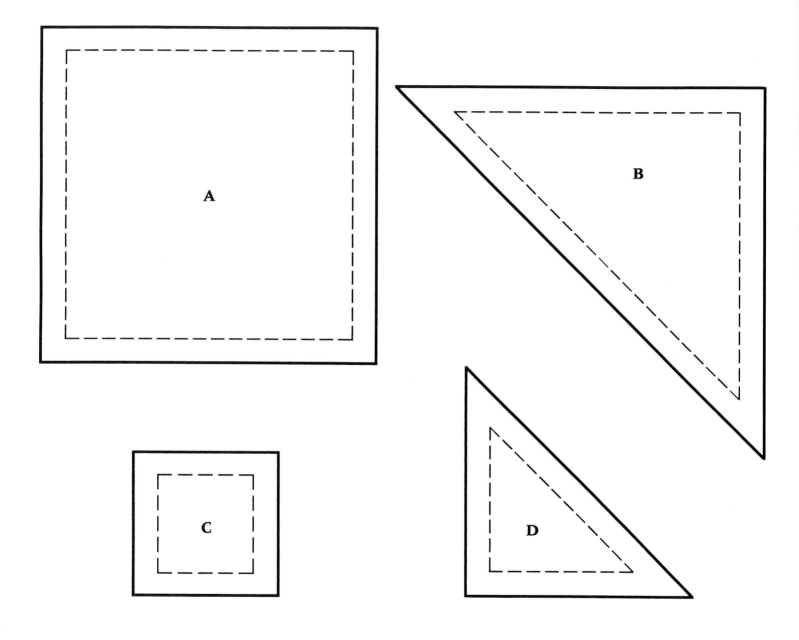

Quilter's Surprise Wallhanging

I enjoy collecting old quilts. For me, there is something warm and wonderful about the soft, worn look of an older quilt and a charm in fabric from the past. I own about 35 quilts that range in age from 50 to 100 years old, and I use them for decorating my house. They are hung on walls, draped over a half-wall in a stairway, and every other place I can find to display them. I even have a quilt on the wall above my bathtub!

The photograph of the Quilter's Surprise project was shot in my living room, where I have an antique fruit-drying hutch filled with some of my quilts. I wanted to design a wallhanging to display above my treasures, and this project is the result.

The wallhanging has two different mini Quilter's Surprise blocks (both made with a single triangle template), and the word "QUILTS" across the center is made of mini letter blocks.

Mini Quilter's Surprise blocks: 4″×4″
Full-size Quilter's Surprise blocks: 12″×12″
Mini letter blocks: 5″×5″ ("I" block: 3″×5″)
Wallhanging: 30″×17″
Seam allowance: ¼″

SUPPLIES

Fabric:
   ¼ yard white solid
   ¼ yard light peach print
   ⅓ yard medium peach print
   ¼ yard light green print
   1 yard medium purple print
   1 yard dark purple solid
   ½ yard desired color, for backing

Batting: ½ yard

Plastic rings, for hanging

CUTTING GUIDE

For Quilter's Surprise Block I (make 6)
  A: 8 white solid
       8 light peach print
       8 medium peach print
       8 dark purple solid

For Quilter's Surprise Block II (make 4)
  A: 4 medium peach print
      16 light green print
      12 medium purple print

For Letter Blocks
Refer to Patchwork Alphabet Quilt (page 199). Follow Cutting Guide for one each of mini letter blocks to spell "QUILTS": Cut all white solid pieces as directed, except omitting #6 pieces for "I" block ("I" will be 3″×5″ instead of 5″×5″). Cut all nonwhite pieces from medium peach print.

Additional Pieces

B (1½″-wide strip):
4 medium purple print, 4½″
2 medium purple print, 5½″
4 medium purple print, 30½″
C (2½″-wide strip): 8 medium purple print, 4½″
Backing: 21½″ × 34½″
Batting: 17½″ × 30½″
Binding: 3 yards dark purple solid

DIRECTIONS

Make ten 4″ × 4″ mini Quilter's Surprise blocks, following step-by-step directions on page 134; make six Block I's and four Block II's.

Make 5″ × 5″ mini "Q," "U" "L," "T," and "S" blocks; make 3″ × 5″ mini "I" block, omitting #6 side pieces; see Patchwork Alphabet Quilt.

To assemble quilt front (see Quilt Diagram): Sew together three Block I's, two Block II's, two 4½″ B's, and four 4½″ C's, to form top row. Assemble bottom row in same manner.

For middle row, stitch letter blocks together, to spell "QUILTS." Stitch 5½″ B's to sides.

Join rows and 30½″ B's, completing quilt front.

To quilt: Set quilt front, batting, and backing together (see "The Quilt Layers," page 14). Referring to "Quilting" (page 15), baste piece for quilting. Quilt around all letters. Make a second row of quilting ⅛″ outside the first row. Continue adding rows ⅛″ apart in this way until the background blocks of the letters are completely quilted. Outline quilt white A's of Quilter's Surprise block I. Quilt around medium peach center and outer edge of medium purple diamond shape of Quilter's Surprise block II. Quilt B strips ⅛″ from binding.

To finish: Trim backing even with quilt front and batting. Bind quilt edges; see "Finishing the Quilt" on page 17. Attach rings for hanging.

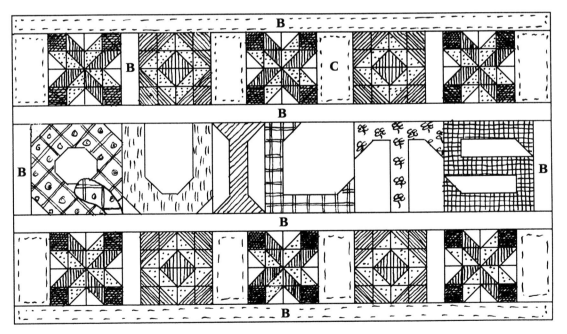

QUILT DIAGRAM

133

Quilter's Surprise Blocks

◆◆◆◆◆◆◆◆◆◆◆◆◆◆◆

Block I

Step 1: Sew together two dark A's, to form a square. (Make 4 dark/dark squares.)

Step 2: Sew together a white A and a light A. (Make 4 white/light squares.)

Step 3: Sew together a white A and a medium A. (Make 4 white/medium squares.)

Step 4: Sew together a light A and a medium A. (Make 4 light/medium squares.)

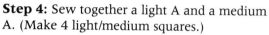

Step 5: Stitch pieced squares together, to form four rows.

Row 1
Row 2
Row 3
Row 4

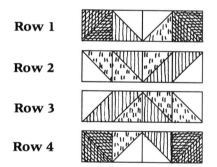

Step 6: Join Rows 1–4, completing the block.

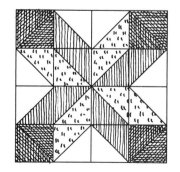

Block II

Step 1: Sew together two light [green] A's, to form a square. (Make 4 light/light squares.)

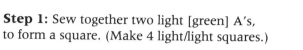

Step 2: Sew together a light [green] A and a medium [purple] A. (Make 8 light/medium squares.)

Step 3: Sew together a medium [purple] A and a medium [peach] A. (Make 4 medium/medium squares.)

Step 4: Stitch pieced squares together, to form four rows.

Row 1
Row 2
Row 3
Row 4

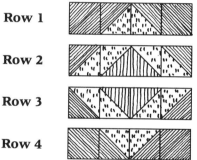

Step 5: Join Rows 1–4, completing the block.

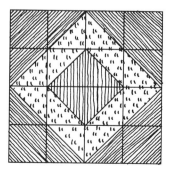

FULL-SIZE QUILTER'S SURPRISE BLOCK TEMPLATE

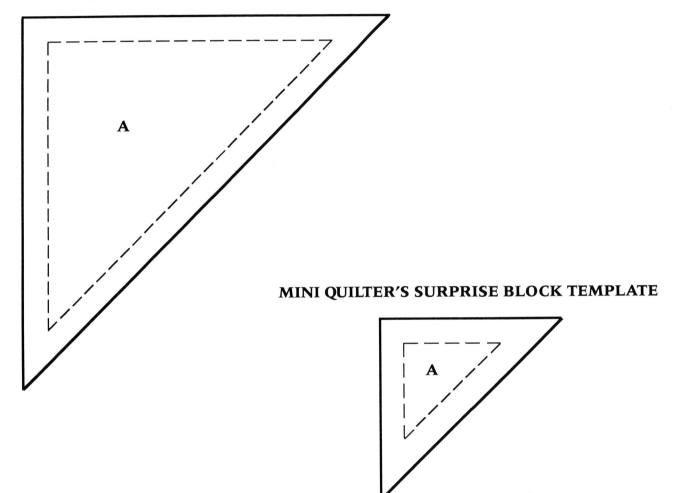

A

MINI QUILTER'S SURPRISE BLOCK TEMPLATE

A

135

Round the Corner Wallhanging

The Round the Corner Wallhanging took shape in a unique way: I designed the project to go with the props, rather than the other way around. I started with the darling little white bed, which I had found at a quilt show, and imagined it as a place for teddy bears to sleep. Eventually I thought of creating the miniature wallhanging to go with it.

Even before I started to sketch the project, I was concerned about finding teddy bears for photography, and I called Colleen Gidner, who designs and collects them. When I went to look through her collection, I took the bed with me, so I could be sure that the bears I chose would be in scale with it. As it turned out, all the teddy bears I selected were ones that Colleen had made.

For the wallhanging itself, I used the simple Round the Corner mini block surrounded by a heavily embroidered border. This is a great take-along project—I worked the embroidery on the sample during a bus tour of Europe, stitching my way through Germany, Austria, and Switzerland.

Mini block: 5″ × 5″
Full-size block: 10″ × 10″
Wallhanging: 7½″ × 9⅝″
Seam allowance: ¼″

SUPPLIES

Fabric:
 ¼ yard white solid
   Scrap of white print
   Scrap of light peach print
   Scrap of medium green print
   Scrap of dark blue print

Embroidery floss:
 1 skein bright peach
 1 skein medium green
 1 skein dark blue

Piping: 1 yard blue

Batting: 8″ × 10″

Plastic rings, for hanging

CUTTING GUIDE

For Round the Corner Block
 A: 4 white print
    4 dark blue print
 B: 8 white print
    4 light peach print
    5 medium green print
    4 dark blue print

Additional Pieces
 Wallhanging shape:
    1 white solid front
    1 white solid backing
    1 batting (minus ¼″ seam allowance)

DIRECTIONS

Make one mini Round the Corner block, following step-by-step directions on this page.

To decorate wallhanging front: Transfer embroidery design and patchwork placement lines to wallhanging front; see "The Quilt Layers," page 14.

Appliqué block on wallhanging front where indicated; see "Appliqué" (page 13).

Work embroidery, following photograph for colors: Use satin stitch to fill flowers, leaves, and ribbons. Work vines in chain stitch. Work letters and stems in backstitch.

To assemble: Prepare piping ends, referring to "Finishing the Quilt" on page 17. Baste piping around wallhanging front on right side, matching raw edges.

Stitch front and backing together, leaving 3" opening in one straight edge for turning; turn to right side. Insert batting through opening, poking it into corners with a knitting needle. Slip-stitch opening closed.

To quilt (See "Quilting," page 15): Quilt around block appliqué and around vines, ribbons, and flowers.

To finish: Attach rings, for hanging.

138

Round the Corner Block
◆◆◆◆◆◆◆◆◆◆◆◆◆◆◆◆◆

Step 1: Sew a white A to a dark A, to form a square. (Make 4 A/A squares.)

Step 2: Stitch pieced and plain squares together, to form five rows.

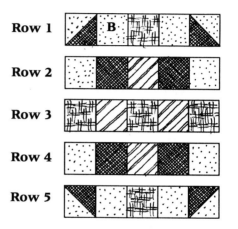

Step 3: Join Rows 1–5, completing the block.

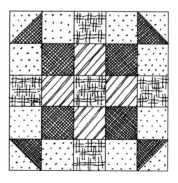

FULL-SIZE ROUND THE CORNER BLOCK TEMPLATES

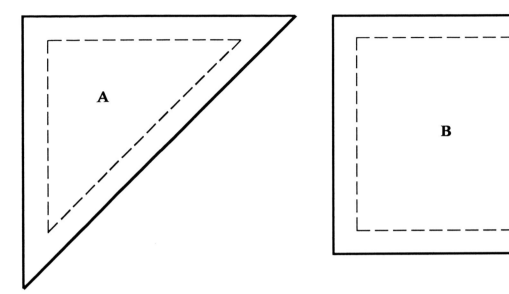

MINI ROUND THE CORNER BLOCK TEMPLATES

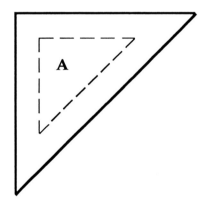

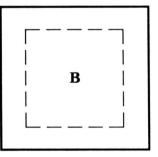

139

patchwork
placement lines

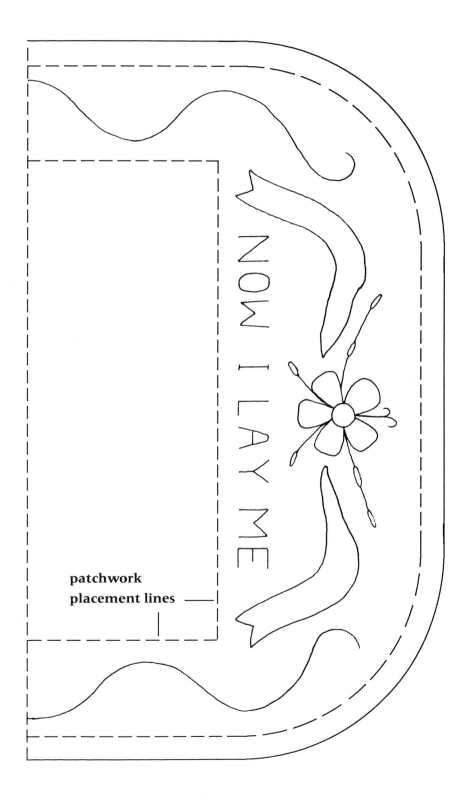

NOW I LAY ME

patchwork
placement lines

141

Schoolhouse Wallhanging

The day I came up with the design for this project, I was on one of my design getaways in Port Townsend, on the shore of the Olympic Peninsula. I had been staying at the Manresa Castle, a Victorian-style bed-and-breakfast with two beautiful turrets and expansive views of the ocean.

I knew from the start that I wanted the "S" project to include a Schoolhouse block, but after puzzling over the design for the better part of a day, I decided to take a break. I drove to Port Townsend's sole movie theater and found that *Driving Miss Daisy* was playing, which I had already seen. A movie about a retired schoolteacher seemed appropriate, so I went in anyway.

When I left the theater, I knew what the project would be: a Schoolhouse wallhanging for Miss Daisy and all teachers everywhere. I worked long into the night with pencil and graph paper, sketching the design. I envisioned the sample just as you see it—made in primary colors, which always remind me of school.

◆◆◆◆◆◆

Full-size Schoolhouse block: 9″ × 9″
Mini letter blocks: 5″ × 5″
Wallhanging: 27½″ × 27½″
Seam allowance: ¼″ (⅛″ for small appliqués)

◆◆◆◆◆◆

SUPPLIES

Fabric:
  ¾ yard white solid
  Scrap of yellow print
  ¼ yard light red solid
  ¼ yard dark red solid
  1 yard dark red print
  Scrap of medium green solid
  ½ yard dark blue print
  1 yard desired color, for backing

Embroidery floss: 1 skein dark green

Batting: 1 yard

Plastic rings, for hanging

CUTTING GUIDE

For Schoolhouse Block
  A: 1 white solid
    1 light red print
    2 dark red solid
  B: 2 white solid
  C: 1 white solid
  D: 2 white solid
  E: 1 dark red solid
  F: 1 light red print
  G: 1 dark red solid
  H: 1 light red print
  I: 3 white solid
    5 dark red solid
  J: 1 dark red solid

K: 1 dark red solid
L: 1 light red print
M: 1 white solid

For Letter Blocks
Refer to Patchwork Alphabet Quilt (page 199). Follow Cutting Guide for four each of mini blocks "A," "B," and "C": Cut all white solid pieces as directed. Cut all nonwhite pieces from dark blue print.

Squares and Strips
A: 4 yellow solid*
N (1½"-wide strip):
    2 dark blue print, 9½"
    2 dark blue print, 11½"
    4 dark red print, 25½"
O (2½"-wide strip): 4 dark red print, 11½"
P: 4 light red print
Q: 4 white solid

Appliqués
Apple: 4 dark red solid
Leaf: 8 medium green solid
Star: 4 yellow solid**

Additional Pieces
Backing: 31½" × 31½"
Batting: 27½" × 27½"
Binding: 1¼ yards dark blue print

Use template A from full-size Schoolhouse block.

**Refer to Independence Square Table Runner and Napkin Rings on page 87. Use Small Star pattern (⅛" seam allowance).*

DIRECTIONS

Make one full-size Schoolhouse block, following step-by-step directions on page 146.

Make four each of mini blocks "A," "B," and "C"; see Patchwork Alphabet Quilt.

For appliqués (see "Appliqué," page 13): Appliqué apples on Q's, referring to Quilt Diagram for placement.

Transfer stem pattern to Q's above apples (see "The Quilt Layers," page 14). Embroider stems solidly with dark green satin stitch.

Appliqué pairs of leaves on Q's with lower edge of one leaf over apple and lower edge of the other under apple. Appliqué stars on P's.

For inner borders: Stitch 9½" N's to top and bottom edges of Schoolhouse block; stitch 11½" N's to sides. Join P's to ends of two O's. Stitch pieced and plain O's to patchwork as for N's.

For "ABC" border: Stitch letter blocks together, to make two horizontal and two vertical "ABC" strips; see Quilt Diagram. Stitch Q's to ends of vertical strips. Stitch horizontal strips to patchwork top and bottom; stitch vertical strips to sides.

For outer border: Stitch A's to ends of two 25½" N's. Stitch plain 25½" N's to patchwork top and bottom; stitch pieced N's to sides.

For quilting: Set quilt front, batting, and backing together. Referring to "Quilting" (page 15), baste piece for quilting. Outline quilt light A's, B's, C's, D's, F's, H's, I's, L's, and M's, as well as the inner edge of N's bordering the schoolhouse. Quilt all four sides of O strips, P and Q blocks, border N strips, and A blocks. Quilt around all patchwork letters, stars, apples, and leaves.

For finishing: Trim backing even with quilt front and batting. Bind quilt edges; see "Finishing the Quilt" on page 17. Attach rings for hanging.

QUILT DIAGRAM

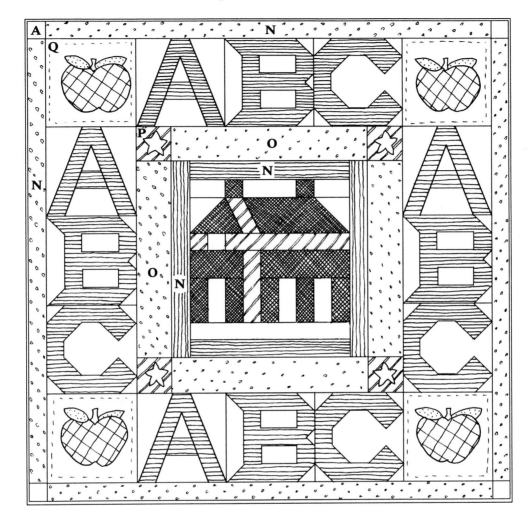

145

Schoolhouse Block

◆◆◆◆◆◆◆◆◆◆◆◆

Step 1: Stitch two dark A's, two white B's, and white C together, to form Row 1.

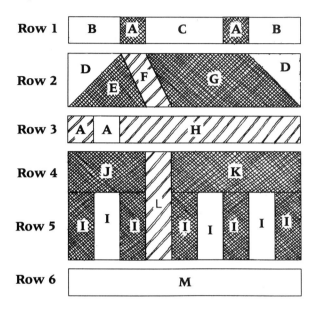

Step 2: Stitch two white D's, dark E, light F, and dark G together, to form Row 2.

Step 3: Stitch light A, white A, and light H together, to form Row 3.

Step 4: Sew together one white I and two dark I's, to form left section of Row 5.

Step 5: Sew together two white I's and three dark I's, to form right section of Row 5.

Step 6: Stitch dark J and K to pieces from Step 5, to form left and right sections of combined Rows 4 and 5.

Step 7: Stitch pieces from Step 6 to light L, to complete Rows 4 and 5.

Step 8: Join Rows 1–6, completing the block.

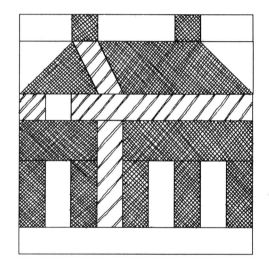

APPLIQUÉ PATTERNS

Leaf

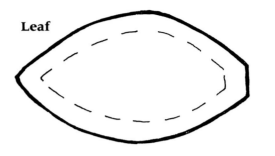

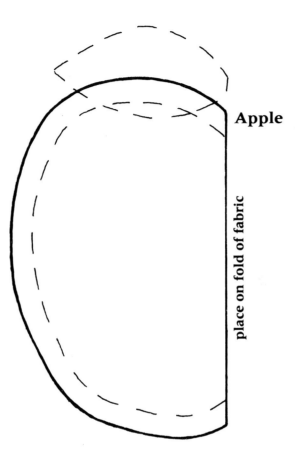

Apple

place on fold of fabric

EMBROIDERY PATTERN

Stem

FULL-SIZE SCHOOLHOUSE BLOCK TEMPLATES

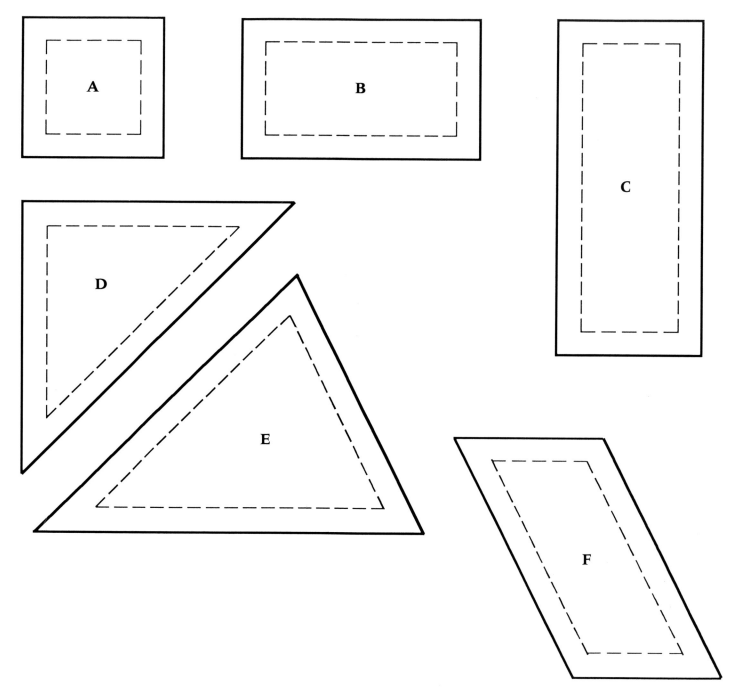

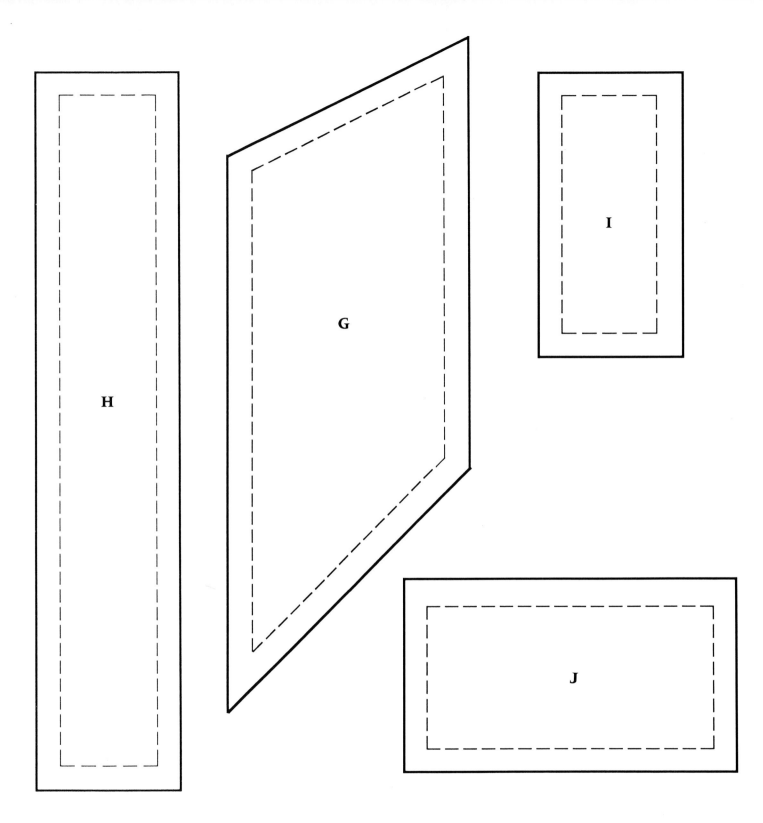

G

H

I

J

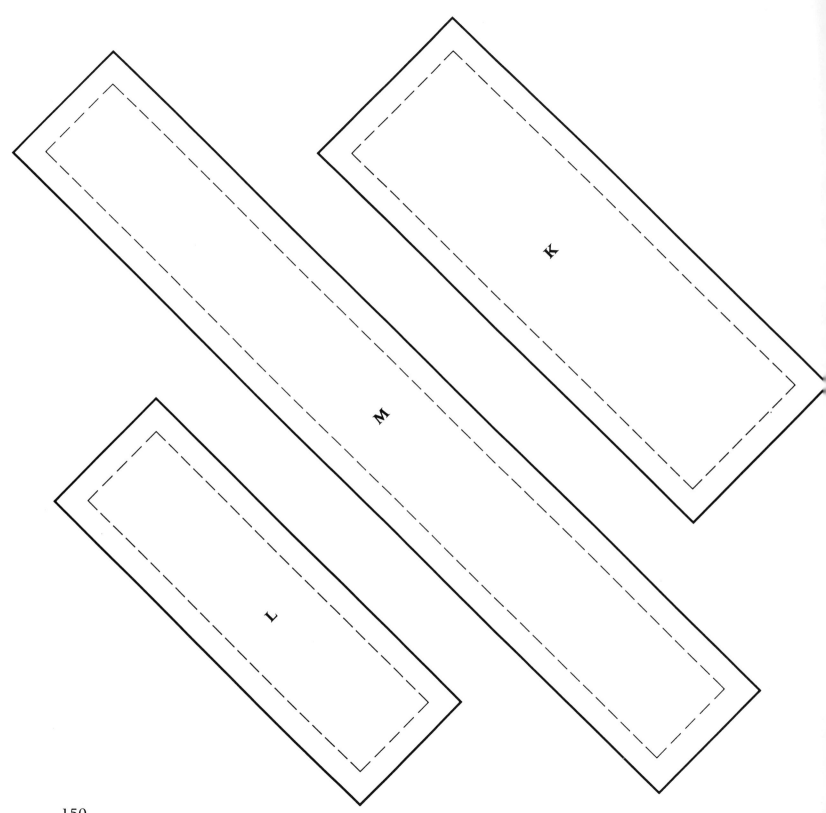

K

M

L

150

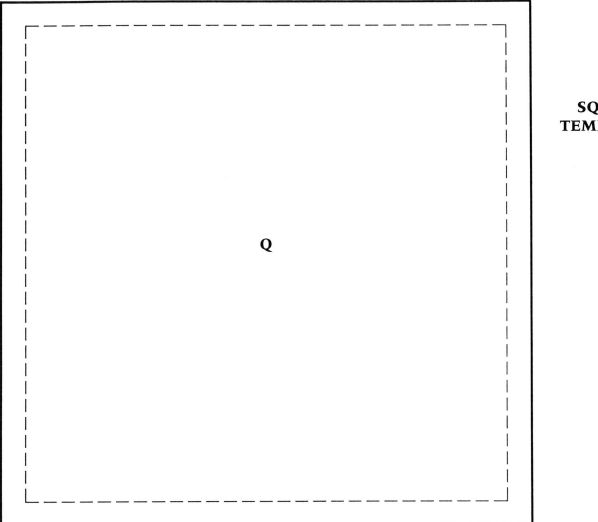

**SQUARE
TEMPLATES**

Q

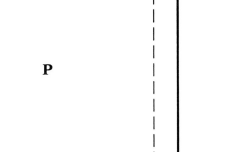

P

Temperance Tree Pillows

The photograph of the Temperance Tree Pillows was shot in my family room, which has not one but two bay windows. I have always loved bay windows—but the seat set into this one was originally covered with an unattractive pea-green vinyl when I first moved in.

From the very beginning, I wanted to have a country print fabric covering the window seat and lots of pillows along the back—some in patchwork and some plain, for contrast. As you can see, I eventually did recover the seat and

make the trio of patchwork pillows that are the "T" project. To complete the look of the room, I covered the camelback loveseat on the opposite wall with the same fabric I used on the window seat and pillows.

The Temperance Tree is a wonderful old pattern that I thought would be a striking design for pillows, and I love the way these three turned out. They would also be attractive accents on a couch or wingback chair.

◆◆◆◆◆◆

Full-size block: 10″ × 10″
Pillow: 14″ × 14″, plus ruffled edging
Seam allowance: ¼

◆◆◆◆◆◆

SUPPLIES
(for 3 pillows)

Fabric:
  ½ yard white solid
  ¼ yard light peach print
  ¼ yard dark green print #1
  2 yards dark green print #2

Batting: ½ yard

Fiberfill

CUTTING GUIDE

For Temperance Tree Block (make 3)
  A: 15 white solid
      2 light peach print
     16 dark green print #1
  B: 2 white solid
  C: 1 light peach print
  D: 2 white solid

Additional Pieces for Each Pillow
  E: 4 dark green print #2
  F (5½″-wide strip): 1¼ yards dark green print #2
  Backing: 14½″ × 14½″ dark green print #2
  Batting: 14½″ × 14½″

DIRECTIONS
(for each pillow)

Make one full-size Temperance Tree block, following step-by-step directions beginning on this page.
  Stitch E's to block sides, completing patchwork pillow front.

  Referring to "Quilting" on page 15, baste batting to wrong side of pillow front for quilting. Quilt outlines of peach A's and D.

To make ruffle: Stitch ends of F together, to form a ring. Fold and press fabric ring in half all around, right side out. Using heavy-duty thread in bobbin, machine-baste ½″ and 1″ from raw ring edges. Pull bobbin threads, gathering fabric to form ruffle to fit around pillow front; secure threads. Arrange gathers evenly, then pin ruffle to right side of pillow front with raw edges even; baste. Stitch ruffle in place.

To assemble: Stitch backing to pillow front, leaving 3″ opening in one edge for turning; turn to right side. Stuff pillow firmly with fiberfill, using a knitting needle to fill corners. Slip-stitch opening closed.

Temperance Tree Block
◆◆◆◆◆◆◆◆◆◆◆◆◆◆◆◆

Step 1: Sew together a light A and a dark A, to form a triangle. (Make 2 light/dark triangles.)

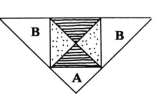

Step 2: Sew together the pieces from Step 1.

Step 3: Stitch one white A and two white B's to the piece from Step 2.

Step 4: Stitch the light C to the piece from Step 3.

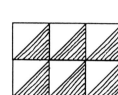

Step 5: Sew together a white A and a dark A, to form a square. (Make 14 white/dark squares.)

Step 6: Stitch six white/dark squares together.

Step 7: Stitch the piece from Step 6 to the piece from Step 4.

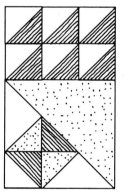

Step 8: Sew together six more white/dark squares.

Step 9: Stitch two white/dark squares and two white D's together.

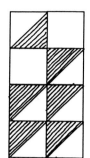

Step 10: Stitch the piece from Step 9 to the piece from Step 8.

Step 11: Stitch the piece from Step 10 to the piece from Step 7, completing the block.

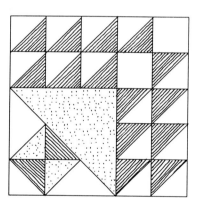

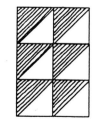

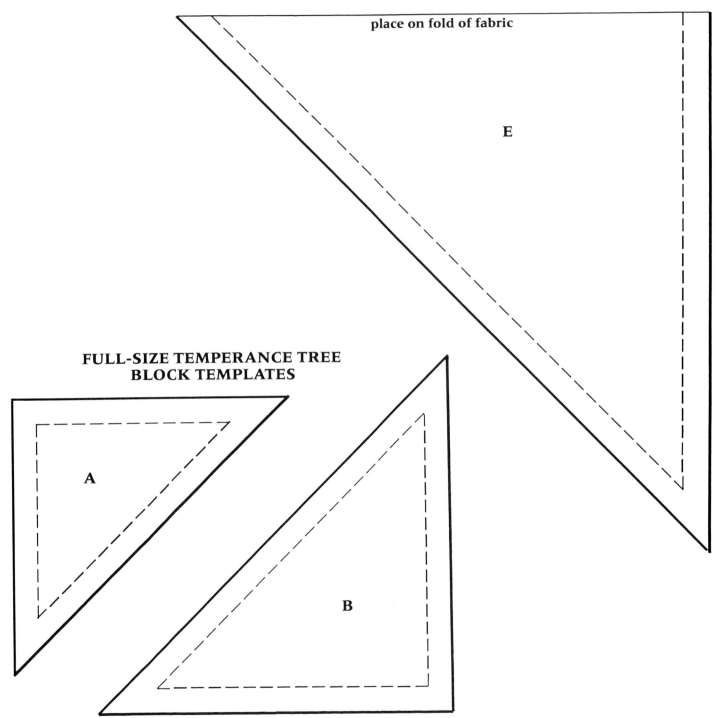

PILLOW CORNER TEMPLATE

place on fold of fabric

E

**FULL-SIZE TEMPERANCE TREE
BLOCK TEMPLATES**

A

B

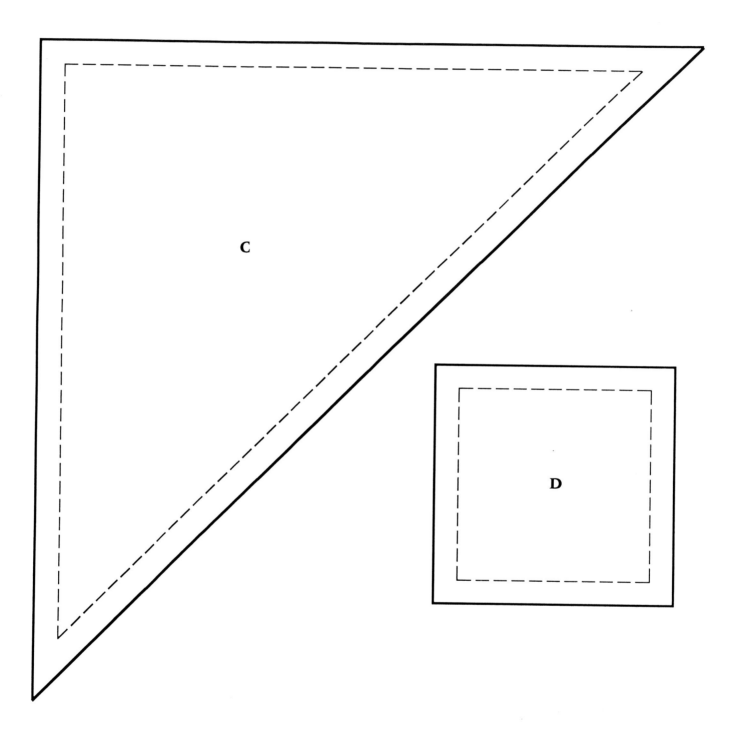

C

D

156

Union Square Mini Quilt and Wallhanging

Here are two projects for Baby's room, both using miniature versions of the Union Square pattern. The blue wallhanging, with "BABY" and a sweet flower embroidered in the center, can be used to decorate a nursery door or wall. The pink quilt, with its double hearts quilted in the center, can be used for holding pins on a changing table or as a coverlet for one of Baby's dolls.

Whatever colors you choose to make them in, these mini patchwork items would be ideal shower gifts for a mother-to-be or as presents for a special little bundle of joy. Quick and easy to make, they are also great take-along projects for times when you want something to keep your hands busy away from home.

Mini block: 6″ × 6″
Full-size block: 12″ × 12″
Quilt: 6″ × 6″
Wallhanging: 6″ × 6″
Seam allowance: ¼″

SUPPLIES
(for mini quilt and wallhanging)

Fabric:
   ¼ yard white solid
   ⅛ yard light pink print
   ⅜ yard dark pink print
   ⅛ yard light blue print
   ⅛ yard dark blue print #1
   ¼ yard dark blue print #2
   ¼ yard desired color, for backing

Embroidery floss:
   1 skein dark pink
   1 skein medium green
   1 skein medium blue
   1 skein yellow

Batting: ¼ yard

Plastic rings, for hanging

CUTTING GUIDE

For Pink Union Square Block
  A: 24 white solid
      16 dark pink print
  B: 4 white solid
      4 light pink print
  C: 4 light pink print

For Blue Union Square Block
  A: 24 white solid
      16 dark blue print #1
  B: 4 white solid
      4 light blue print
  C: 4 light blue print

Additional Pieces for Quilt
  Backing: 6½″ × 6½″

Batting: 6½" × 6½"
Binding: ¾ yard dark pink print

Additional Pieces for Wallhanging
Backing: 6½" × 6½"
Batting: 6½" × 6½"
Binding: ¾ yard dark blue print #2

DIRECTIONS

Mini Quilt

Make one pink mini Union Square block, following step-by-step directions beginning on this page.

Transfer double-heart quilting motif to center four B's (see "The Quilt Layers," page 14).

Set quilt front, batting, and backing together. Referring to "Quilting" (page 15), baste piece for quilting. Quilt heart motif.

Bind quilt edges; see "Finishing the Quilt" on page 17. Attach rings for hanging.

Mini Wallhanging

Make one blue mini Union Square block.

Transfer embroidery pattern for "BABY" and floral design to center four B's.

Use green floss to work vines in backstitch and to fill leaves with satin stitch. Fill in flower petals with red satin stitch and flower center with yellow satin stitch.

Set quilt front, batting, and backing together; baste. Bind quilt edges.

Union Square Block

◆◆◆◆◆◆◆◆◆◆◆◆◆◆

Step 1: Stitch two white A's to a light B.

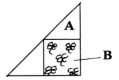

Step 2: Stitch a light C to the piece from Step 1.

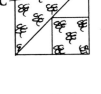

Step 3: Sew together a white A and a dark A, to form a square. (Make 4 A/A squares.)

Step 4: Stitch two A/A squares together.

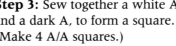

Step 5: Stitch piece from Step 4 to piece from Step 2.

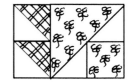

Step 6: Stitch two A/A squares and a white B together.

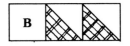

Step 7: Join pieces from Steps 5 and 6, to complete the quarter-block.

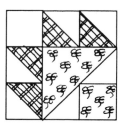

Step 8: Make three more quarter-blocks, following Steps 1–7.

Step 9: Join the four quarter-blocks, completing the block.

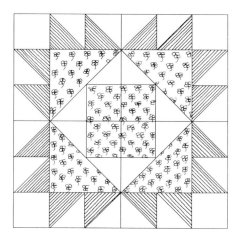

QUILTING MOTIF

EMBROIDERY PATTERN

FULL-SIZE UNION SQUARE BLOCK TEMPLATES

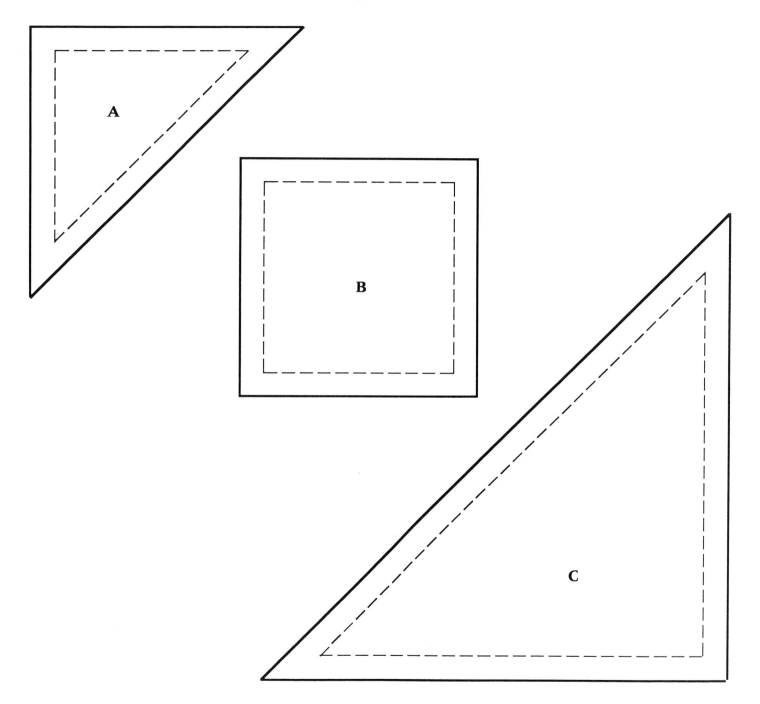

MINI UNION SQUARE BLOCK TEMPLATES

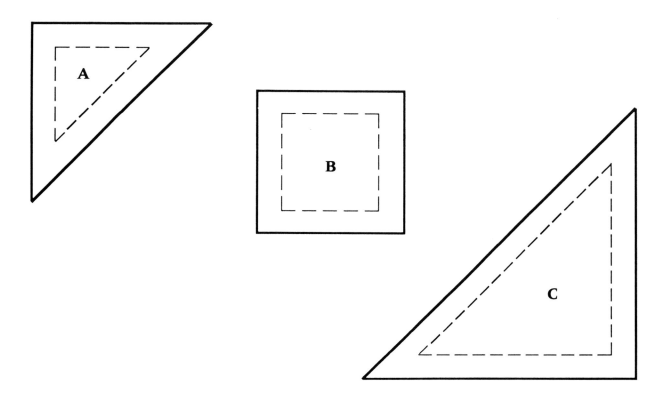

Variable Star and Magnolia Bud Wallhanging

I originally designed the Variable Star and Magnolia Bud Wallhanging with pieced blocks in the main body only. I liked the way the corner buds pointed toward the dark center block, but it looked as though something was missing. After a while, I came up with the idea of adding the mini stars-and-buds border, and then the wallhanging finally looked complete.

I gave the sample for this project to my mother when she was redecorating her family room. She likes pinks, blues, and yellows, and I thought that this wallhanging would be a nice addition to her home. My mother agreed. She chose wallpaper for the family room that had pink and blue flowers on a light yellow background (which took me only a day and a half to install—and it looks great!). Then she added accessories to coordinate with both the paper and the wallhanging.

You can make this project to enhance a room of your own—or you can give it to somebody special, as I did.

◆◆◆◆◆◆

Mini blocks: 4″ × 4″
Full-size blocks: 8″ × 8″
Wallhanging: 36″ × 36″
Seam allowance: ¼″

◆◆◆◆◆◆

SUPPLIES

Fabric:
- 1¼ yards white solid
- ¼ yard light yellow solid
- 1¼ yards dark pink solid
- Scrap of medium blue print #1
- ¼ yard medium blue print #2
- ½ yard dark blue solid
- 1¼ yards dark green print
- 1¼ yards desired color, for backing

Embroidery floss: 1 skein dark pink

Batting: 1⅛ yards

Plastic rings, for hanging

CUTTING GUIDE

For Dark-Value Full-Size Variable Star Block
- A: 8 dark blue solid
- B: 2 light yellow solid
  - 2 medium blue print #1
- C: 8 white solid
  - 4 dark pink solid
  - 8 dark blue solid
- D: 4 white solid

For Medium-Value Full-Size Variable Star Block (make 4)
- A: 8 dark pink solid
- B: 2 light yellow solid
  - 2 medium blue print #1

C: 8 white solid
12 medium blue print #2
D: 4 white solid

For Mini Variable Star Block (make 16)

E: 8 white solid
8 dark pink solid
F: 4 white solid
2 light yellow solid
2 dark green print

For Full-Size Magnolia Bud Block (make 4)

G: 1 white solid
1 light yellow solid
H: 1 white solid
I: 4 white solid (2 reversed)
2 dark pink solid (1 reversed)
2 dark green print (1 reversed)
J: 3 white solid
K: 1 dark pink solid

For Mini Magnolia Bud Block (make 8)

F: 4 white solid*
L: 4 white solid (2 reversed)
2 light yellow solid (1 reversed)
2 dark green print (1 reversed)
M: 1 light yellow solid

Additional Pieces

N (1½"-wide strip):
24 dark blue solid, 4½"
2 dark blue solid, 24½"
2 dark blue solid, 26½"
2 dark blue solid, 34½"
2 dark blue solid, 36½"
Backing: 40½" × 40½"
Batting: 36½" × 36½"
Binding: 4¼ yards dark pink solid

Use template F from Mini Variable Star block.

DIRECTIONS

Make a dark-value full-size Variable Star block, following step-by-step directions on page 168. Make four medium-value full-size Variable Star blocks in same manner, substituting medium blue C's for all nonwhite C's.

Make 16 mini Variable Star blocks, four full-size Magnolia Bud blocks, and eight mini Magnolia Bud blocks as follows.

Mini Variable Star Block (make 16)

Step 1: Sew together a white E and a dark E, to form a square. (Make 8 white/dark squares.)

Step 2: Stitch pieced and plain squares together, to form four rows.

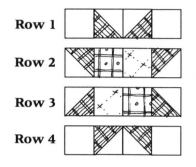

Row 1

Row 2

Row 3

Row 4

Step 3: Join Rows 1–4 completing the block.

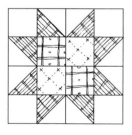

Full-Size Magnolia Bud Block (make 4)

Step 1: Stitch G's together.

G

Step 2: Stitch H to piece from Step 1.

H

Step 3: Sew together a white I and a dark pink I, to form a rectangle.

Step 4: Make another white/pink rectangle, using reversed I's.

Step 5: Sew together a white I and a dark green I, to form a rectangle.

Step 6: Make another white/green rectangle, using reversed I's.

Step 7: Stitch pieced and plain squares and rectangles together, to form three rows.

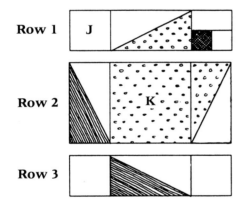

Step 8: Join Rows 1–3, completing the block.

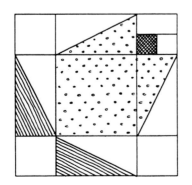

Mini Magnolia Bud Block (make 8)

Step 1: Mark a square in one corner of an F; embroider solidly with dark pink satin stitch.

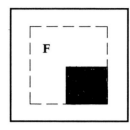

Step 2: Sew together a white L and a light L, to form a rectangle.

Step 3: Make another white/light rectangle, using reversed L's.

Step 4: Sew together a white L and dark L, to form a rectangle.

Step 5: Make another white/dark rectangle, using reversed L's.

Step 6: Stitch squares and rectangles together, to form three rows.

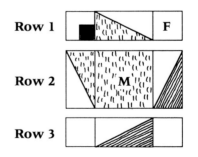

166

Step 7: Join Rows 1–3, completing the block.

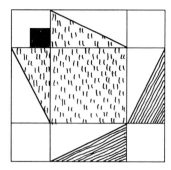

Assembling the Quilt Front

Stitch full-size blocks together, to form three rows with three blocks in each row; see Quilt Diagram. Join rows.

Stitch 24½" N's to top and bottom edges of patchwork; stitch 26½" N's to sides.

For outer borders: Sew together mini blocks and 4½" N's, to form two horizontal and two vertical border strips; see Quilt Diagram. Stitch horizontal pieced strips to patchwork top and bottom; stitch vertical pieced strips to sides.

Stitch 34½" N's to top and bottom quilt edges; stitch 36½" N's to sides.

Quilting

Set quilt front, batting, and backing together (see "The Quilt Layers," page 15). Referring to "Quilting" (page 15), baste piece for quilting. Quilt around the five large Variable Star blocks; also quilt the center A's, D's, and C's of each block. In the large Magnolia Bud blocks, quilt around each flower and leaf. Quilt around the stars and flowers on all border blocks.

Finishing

Trim backing even with quilt front and batting. Bind quilt edges; see "Finishing the Quilt" on page 17. Attach rings for hanging.

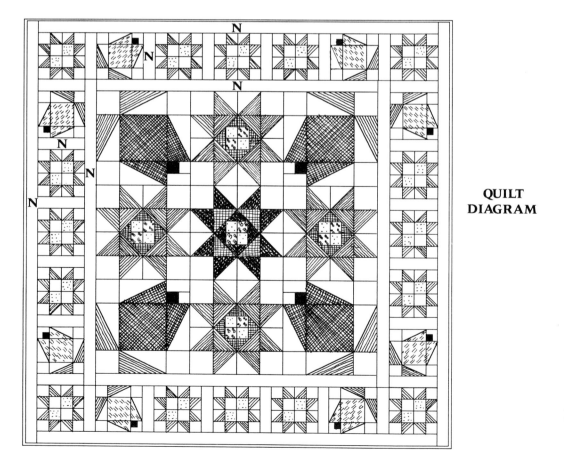

QUILT DIAGRAM

167

Variable Star Block

◆◆◆◆◆◆◆◆◆◆◆◆◆

Step 1: Stitch two dark A's to a medium [blue] B, to form a triangle. (Make 2 dark/medium triangles.)

Step 2: Stitch two dark A's to a light [yellow] B, to form a triangle. (Make 2 dark/light triangles.)

Step 3: Stitch a dark [pink] C to each triangle from Steps 1 and 2.

Step 4: Sew together a white C and a dark [blue] C, to form a square. (Make 8 squares.)

Step 6: Join Rows 1–4, completing the block.

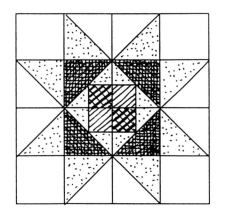

Step 5: Stitch pieced and plain squares together, to form four rows.

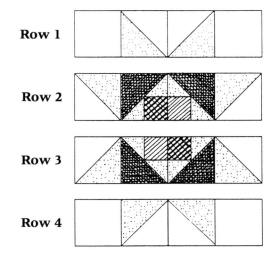

168

FULL-SIZE VARIABLE STAR BLOCK TEMPLATES

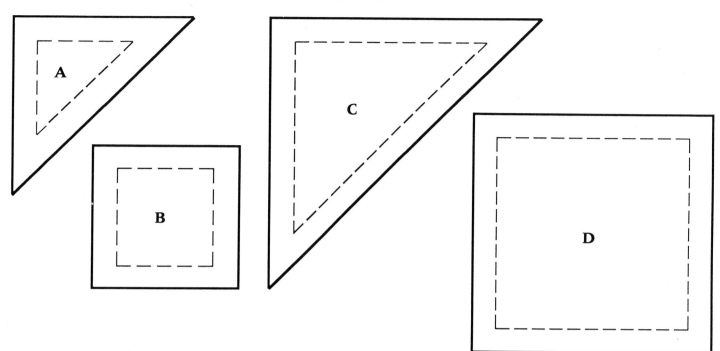

FULL-SIZE MAGNOLIA BUD BLOCK TEMPLATES

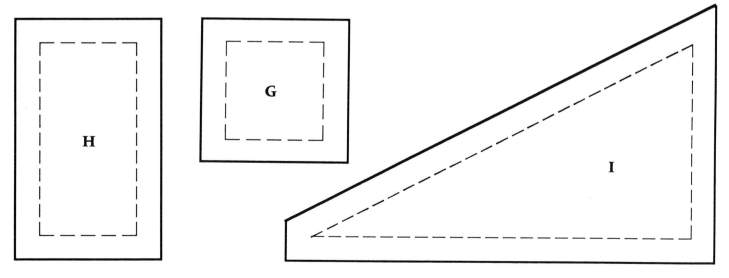

169

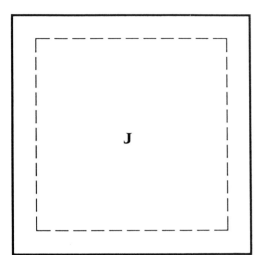

J

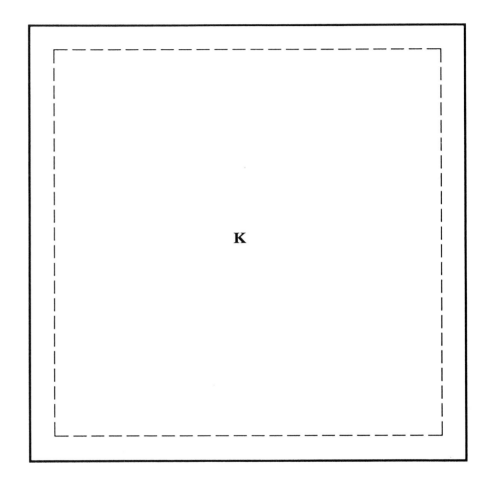

K

170

MINI VARIABLE STAR BLOCK TEMPLATES

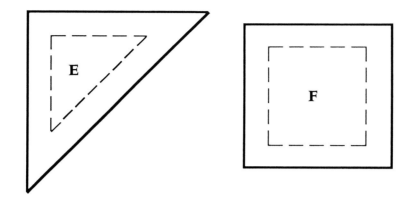

MINI MAGNOLIA BUD BLOCK TEMPLATES

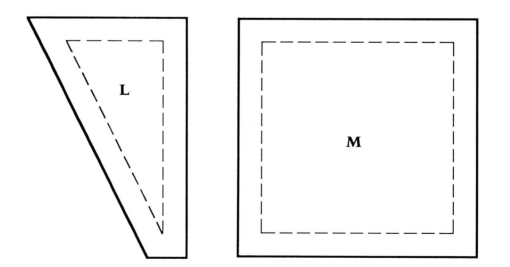

Windblown Square Quilt

The photograph of this project was taken on the rear deck of my house in the summertime. The deck looks out onto a pond, which usually has ducks swimming playfully around in it.

In the Pacific Northwest where I live, no matter how hot the days of summer are, the nights are always cold. (I have seen T-shirts that say, "The best winter I ever had was the summer I spent in Seattle.") I have spent many a Fourth of July night shivering in a coat as I watched the local fireworks display. I designed this project as a quilt that I could use on my deck on those chilly summer evenings.

The Windblown Square pattern reminds me of a boat with white sails being blown around on a blustery day. The energetic feel of the design is produced by an interplay of colors and not by a lot of differently shaped pieces: The full-size blocks are made using only one template, a triangle. The mini nine-patches set into the corners of the yellow-and-white striped border also use only one template, a square.

Full-size block: 12″ × 12″
Mini nine-patch: 3″ × 3″
Quilt: 72″ × 84″
Seam allowance: ¼″

SUPPLIES

Fabric:
- 2 yards white solid
- ½ yard dark yellow solid
- ¾ yard light blue solid
- 1½ yards medium blue print
- ¾ yard dark blue print #1
- 2 yards dark blue print #2
- 5 yards desired color, for backing

Batting: 4¼ yards

CUTTING GUIDE

For Windblown Square Block (make 30)
- A: 12 white solid
  - 4 light blue solid
  - 8 medium blue print
  - 8 dark blue print #1

For Nine-Patch (make 4)
- B: 5 white solid
  - 4 dark blue print #1

Additional Pieces
- C (1½″-wide strip):
  - 2 white solid, 60½″
  - 2 white solid, 72½″
  - 4 dark yellow solid, 60½″
  - 4 dark yellow solid, 72½″
- D (3½″-wide strip):
  - 2 medium blue print, 66½″
  - 2 medium blue print, 84½″

Backing: 76½" × 88½"
Batting: 72½" × 84½"
Binding: 9¼ yards dark blue print #2

DIRECTIONS

Make 30 full-size Windblown Square blocks, following step-by-step directions beginning on this page.

Make four mini nine-patches as follows.

Nine-Patch (make 4)

Step 1: Stitch B's together, to form three rows.

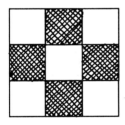

Step 2: Join Rows 1–3, completing the block.

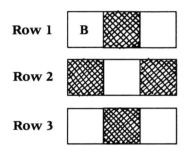

Assembling the Quilt Front

Stitch Windblown Square blocks together to form six rows with five blocks in each row. Join rows.

Stitch one white 60½" C between two yellow 60½" C's, side by side, to form top striped border piece (see photograph). Assemble bottom striped border piece in same manner. Assemble side striped border pieces, using 72½"

C's. Stitch nine patches to ends of side pieces. Sew shorter striped pieces to top and bottom edges of patchwork; sew longer striped pieces to sides.

Stitch shorter D's to quilt top and bottom; stitch longer D's to sides.

Quilting

Transfer tulip motif to center of each Windblown Square block; see "The Quilt Layers," page 14.

Set quilt front, batting, and backing together. Referring to "Quilting" (page 15), baste piece for quilting. Quilt tulip motifs. Quilt around the large diamond of each Windblown Square block. To quilt the borders, outline the white B's in the four corner nine-patches and the white C strips.

Finishing

Trim backing even with quilt front and batting. Bind quilt edges; see "Finishing the Quilt" on page 17.

Windblown Square Block
◆◆◆◆◆◆◆◆◆◆◆◆◆◆◆◆◆◆◆

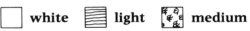 white   light   medium   dark

Step 1: Sew together a white A and a light A, to form a square. (Make 4 white/light squares.)

Step 2: Sew together a white A and a medium A. (Make 4 white/medium squares.)

Step 3: Sew together a white A and a dark A. (Make 4 white/dark squares.)

Step 4: Sew together a light A and a dark A. (Make 4 medium/dark squares.)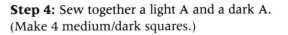

Step 5: Stitch pieced squares together, to form four rows.

Row 1
Row 2
Row 3
Row 4

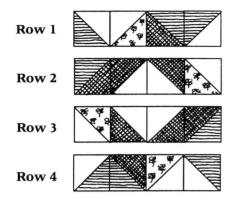

Step 6: Join Rows 1–4, completing the block.

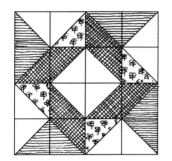

QUILTING MOTIF

FULL-SIZE WINDBLOWN SQUARE
BLOCK TEMPLATE

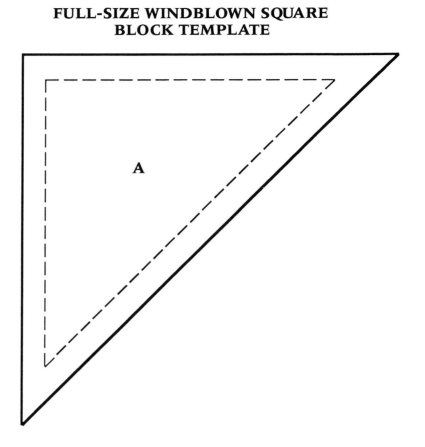

A

MINI NINE-PATCH TEMPLATE

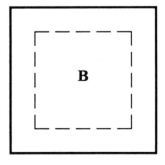

B

X-Quartet Towel

Because I love quilting so much, I like to have as many quilts around my house as possible. I also enjoy seeing little bits of patchwork here, there, and everywhere—especially in unexpected places.

The X-Quartet Towel is a quick and easy project that looks as though a lot more effort goes into its construction than actually does. For a minimal amount of work, you can put this little bit of patchwork in your kitchen, where it would be an attractive dish towel, hand towel, or decorative piece. It might also be fun to make a pair of towels for a bride-to-be as a shower gift in her favorite colors.

◆◆◆◆◆◆

Mini block: 4″ × 4″
Full-size block: 12″ × 12″
Towel: 20″ × 28″
Seam allowance: ¼″

◆◆◆◆◆◆

SUPPLIES

Fabric:
    Scrap of white solid
    Scrap of light red print
    Scrap of medium red print
    Scrap of dark red solid

Double-fold bias tape: 1½ yards red, ¼″ wide
Cotton towel: 20″ × 28″ dark blue/white striped

CUTTING GUIDE

For X-Quartet Block
  A: 8 white solid
     4 light red print
     4 medium red print
  B: 4 white solid
     4 dark red solid

Additional Pieces
  C: 2 bias-tape strips, 4¼″
  D: 2 bias-tape strips, 4½″
  E: 2 bias-tape strips, 4½″ shorter than towel
     width

DIRECTIONS

Make one mini X-Quartet block, following step-by-step directions on page 179.

Appliqué

Appliqué block on towel (see "Appliqué," page 13) 2½″ up from bottom, referring to photograph for placement.

Appliqué strips on towel as follows, being sure to pin all pieces in place before stitching.

Step 1: Mark diagonal and horizontal guidelines on towel.

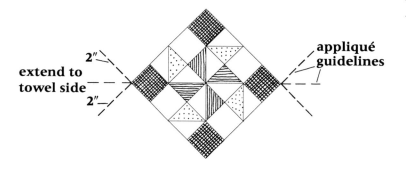

Step 2: Pin a C above upper left side of block.

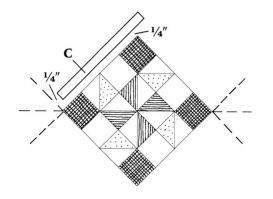

Step 3: Pin a D above upper right side of block, folding excess at top smoothly around and under C.

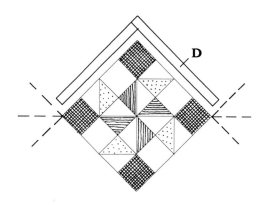

Step 4: Pin an E above left horizontal guideline, folding excess at inner end smoothly around and under C; fold under opposite end, so that it is even with side edge of towel; pin.

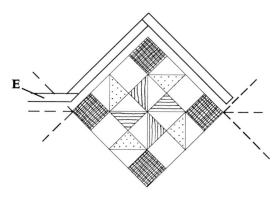

Step 5: Pin an E above right horizontal guideline.

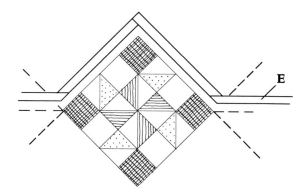

Step 6: Rotate towel and pin strips below block, following Steps 2–5.

Step 7: Appliqué all strips in place.

X-Quartet Block

◆◆◆◆◆◆◆◆◆◆◆

Step 1: Sew together a white A and a light A, to form a square. (Make 4 white/light squares.)

Step 2: Sew together a white A and a medium A. (Make 4 white/medium squares.)

Step 3: Stitch pieced and plain squares together, to form four rows.

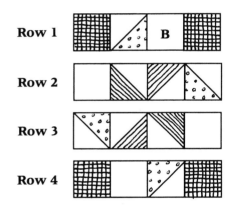

Row 1

Row 2

Row 3

Row 4

Step 4: Join Rows 1–4, completing the block.

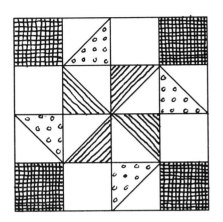

FULL-SIZE X-QUARTET BLOCK TEMPLATES

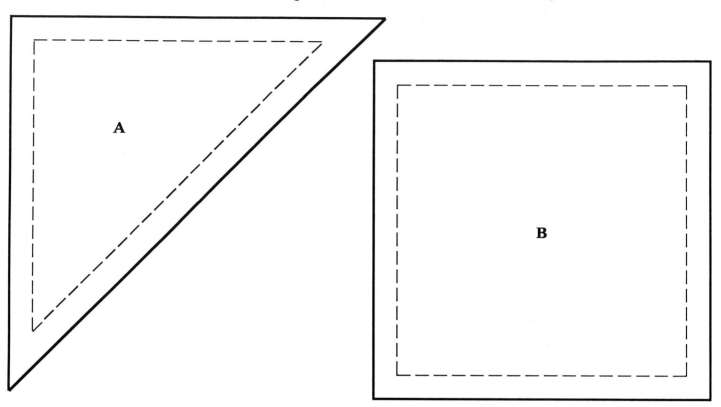

MINI X-QUARTET BLOCK TEMPLATES

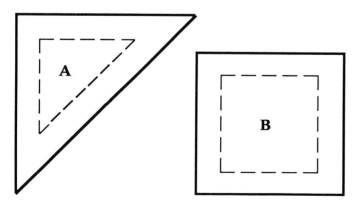

Young Man's Fancy Tablecloth and Chair Back

Patchwork tablecloths have always seemed charming to me. Some years ago, I found a design in a magazine for a tablecloth with a patchwork Christmas tree pattern. I loved the look of the sample, so I saved the instructions for making it and one day I was finally inspired to stitch up one of my own.

Every year since then, I have displayed my patchwork tablecloth on a table in the entryway of my house with a small Christmas tree on top—and I have always felt a little twinge of sadness when, after the holidays were over, I packed away my special tablecloth for another year.

I designed this project so that I could have a patchwork tablecloth in my home year-round. I used the Young Man's Fancy pattern (I love the mini nine-patches that are part of the full-size block) and some of my favorite colors. You can use your favorite colors for making this patchwork tablecloth and chair back set that is pretty but practical enough for every day of the year.

◆◆◆◆◆◆

Full-size block: 15″ × 15″
Tablecloth: 34½″ × 34½″, plus lace edging
Chair back: 17″ × 18″, plus piping
Seam allowance: ¼″

◆◆◆◆◆◆

SUPPLIES
(for tablecloth and one chair back)

Fabric:
    2 yards white solid
    1¾ yards dark coral print
    1 medium green print

Cotton eyelet lace: 4 yards white, ½″ wide

Piping: 2¼ yards white

Batting: ½ yard

CUTTING GUIDE

For Young Man's Fancy Block (make 5)
  A: 20 white solid
      16 dark coral print
  B: 4 white solid
      8 medium green print
  C: 12 white solid
      12 medium green print
  D: 5 white solid

Additional Pieces for Tablecloth
  E (2″-wide strip):
      2 dark coral print, 15½″
      3 dark coral print, 32″
      2 dark coral print, 35″
  Backing: 35″ × 35″ white solid

Additional Pieces for Chair Back
E (2"-wide strip): 2 dark coral print, 15½"
F (1½"-wide strip): 2 dark coral print, 18½"
Ties (1"-wide strip): 4 dark coral print, 21"
Backing: 17½" × 18½" dark coral print
Batting: 17" × 18"

DIRECTIONS

Make five full-size Young Man's Fancy blocks, following step-by-step directions on page 184.

Tablecloth

Assemble tablecloth front as follows.

Step 1: Stitch two blocks to a 15½" E. (Make two pieces.)

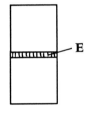

Step 2: Stitch pieces to a 32" E.

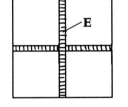

Step 3: Stitch two 32" E's to patchwork sides.

Step 4: Stitch 35" E's to top and bottom.

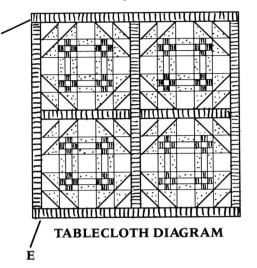

TABLECLOTH DIAGRAM

For lace: Press one end of lace ½" to wrong side. Beginning in center of one edge of tablecloth front with pressed end of lace, pin lace around patchwork with right sides together, ruffles facing in, and outer edges even; overlap ends; baste.

For backing: Stitch backing to tablecloth front, right sides together, leaving 3" opening in one edge for turning; turn to right side. Slip-stitch opening closed.

Chair Back

Stitch E's to top and bottom of one block; stitch F's to sides.

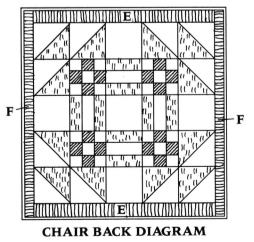

CHAIR BACK DIAGRAM

For piping: Prepare piping ends; see "Finishing the Quilt" on page 18. Baste piping all around one patchwork block on right side of fabric with raw (outer) edges even.

For ties: For each tie, press long edges of fabric to wrong side, so that they meet along center of strip. Press strip in half lengthwise along center, hiding long raw edges and matching previous folds; stitch close to folds. Knot each end of tie; trim away excess fabric close to knots.

Press ties in half widthwise; pin in place on top and bottom (shorter) edges of patchwork ½″ in from each corner; folded edges of ties should be even with raw edges of piping and patchwork, with knots facing inward; baste. Pin tie ends to fabric, so that they won't get caught in stitching.

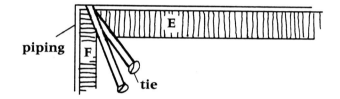

For backing: Stitch backing to patchwork front, right sides together, leaving 3″ opening in one edge for turning; turn to right side. Remove pins securing tie ends.

For batting: Insert batting through opening, poking it into corners with a knitting needle.

For quilting (see "Quilting," page 15): Baste piece for quilting. Quilt around pieced squares of block and along inner and outer edges of E/F border.

Young Man's Fancy Block

Step 1: Sew together five white A's and four dark A's, to form a checkered square. (Make 4 checkered squares.)

Step 2: Stitch two medium B's to a white B, to make a striped square. (Make 4 striped squares.)

Step 3: Sew together a white C and a medium C, to form a square. (Make 12 C/C squares.)

Step 4: Stitch pieced and plain squares together, to form five rows.

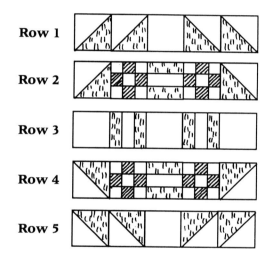

Step 5: Join Rows 1–5, completing the block.

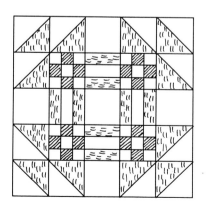

184

FULL-SIZE YOUNG MAN'S FANCY BLOCK TEMPLATES

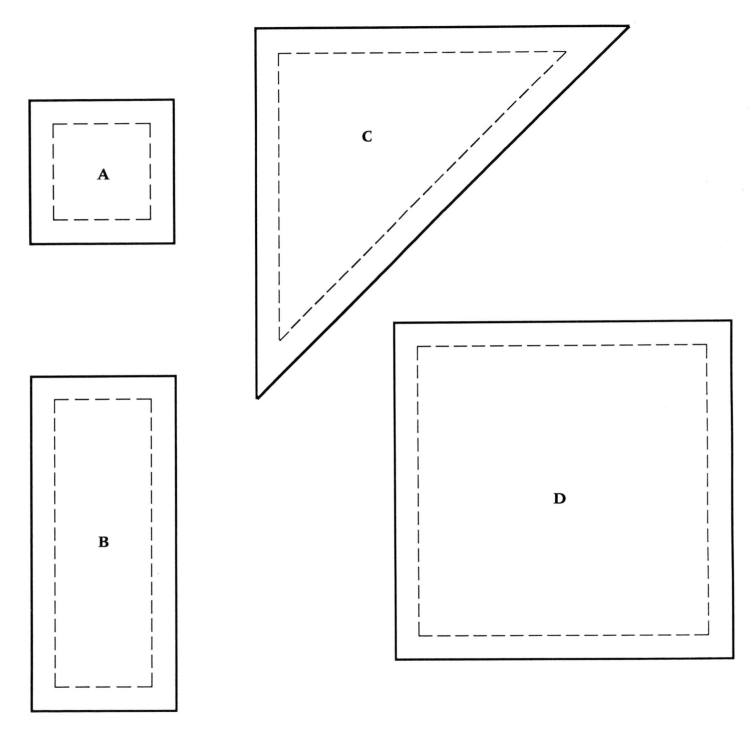

Z-Cross Christmas Stocking

When I was growing up, my Christmas stocking was often one of my dad's stretch-nylon socks. The year that I became engaged to be married, I designed and made a special Christmas stocking (one that would never suit my taste now) for my fiancé. It was made of felt and had cute holiday shapes that I decorated with sequins. I added the name of my husband-to-be across the top of the stocking by gluing on cutout felt letters that spelled "JOHN."

These days I prefer patchwork stockings. I have seen several made from "cutter quilts"; that is, stocking fronts that were cut from an old quilt and then stitched to a plain fabric back. While I love the look of quilting, I cringe at the thought of any quilt, especially an old one, being cut up, so I designed this patchwork-adorned stocking instead.

The mini block is made in the Z-Cross pattern and then appliquéd on the stocking front, which is embellished with embroidered holly leaves and berries. I like the sample so much that I just might keep it to hang on my very own mantel next Christmas!

Mini block: 5″ × 5″
Full-size block: 10″ × 10″
Stocking: 11″ × 17″, plus lace edging
Seam allowance: ¼″

SUPPLIES

Fabric:
     Scrap of white solid
⅔ yard light cream print
     Scrap of bright red print
     Scrap of dark green solid
     Scrap of medium red/green print

Embroidery floss:
  1 skein bright red
  1 skein dark green

Ribbon: 4″ red, ¼″ wide

Cotton eyelet lace: ½ yard white, 1½″ wide

Batting: ⅓ yard

CUTTING GUIDE

For Z-Cross Block
  A: 8 white solid
       8 medium red/green print
  B: 5 white solid
       4 bright red print
       8 dark green solid

Additional Pieces
Stocking*
Batting**
Toe: 1 bright red print
Heel: 1 bright red print

*Enlarge stocking pattern on ½" squares (see "Templates and Patterns" on page 21), adding ¼" seam allowance all around shape. Use enlarged pattern to cut four stocking shapes from light cream print (reversing two of them).

**Use enlarged stocking pattern to cut one shape from batting. Trim away ¼" seam allowance all around batting shape.

DIRECTIONS

Make one mini Z-Cross block, following step-by-step directions on opposite page.

Mark a 5" × 5" square (patchwork placement lines) on right side of one left-pointing stocking (stocking front), referring to pattern on grid for placement.

Transfer actual-size embroidery designs for "MERRY" and holly above and below marked square (see "The Quilt Layers," page 14), being sure to leave seam allowances unmarked.

To appliqué (see "Appliqué" on page 13): Press straight edges of Z-Cross block, heel, and toe ¼" to wrong side. Appliqué block on stocking front. Pin heel and toe in place; appliqué along straight edges only. Baste curved edges of heel and toe to seam allowance of stocking, to secure.

To embroider: Use green floss to embroider letters in chain stitch and holly leaves in satin stitch. Fill berries solidly in satin stitch with red.

To quilt: Pin batting shape to wrong side of stocking front, centered; baste piece for quilting (see "Quilting" on page 15). Quilt around patchwork appliqué and embroidered holly. Quilt straight edges of appliquéd heel and toe.

To assemble stocking: Baste stocking front and one reversed stocking shape (stocking back) together, right sides in. Stitch side and bottom edges, leaving top straight edge open; turn to right side.

To attach lace and hanging loop: Press one end of lace ½" to wrong side. Beginning in center of top edge of stocking back with folded end of lace, baste lace around outside of stocking top, right sides together, matching raw (upper) edges; overlap ends. Stitch lace in place.

Fold ribbon in half, to form 2"-long hanging loop. Stitch loop to top edge of stocking back over lace, so that loop faces downward and cut ends are even with upper edges of fabric and lace.

Press upper edge of stocking ¼" to inside; hanging loop and lace will extend above stocking.

To assemble lining: Stitch remaining stocking shapes (lining front and back) together at side and bottom edges; do not turn to right side. Press top straight edge of lining ¼" to outside.

Insert lining into stocking, matching seams and folded edges. Hand-sew lining to stocking along top edge with tiny, invisible stitches.

Z-Cross Block

◆◆◆◆◆◆◆◆◆

Step 1: Sew together a white A and a medium A, to form a square. (Make 8 white/medium squares.)

Step 2: Stitch pieced and plain squares together, to form five rows.

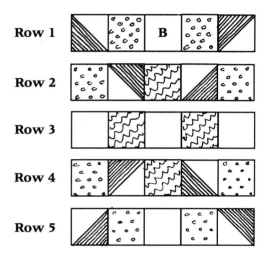

Step 3: Join Rows 1–5, completing the block.

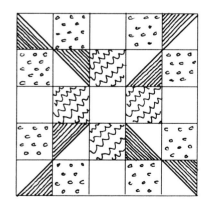

STOCKING PATTERN

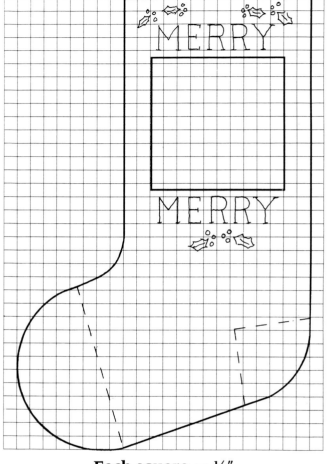

Each square = ½″

189

EMBROIDERY PATTERNS

Holly

MERRY

APPLIQUÉ PATTERNS

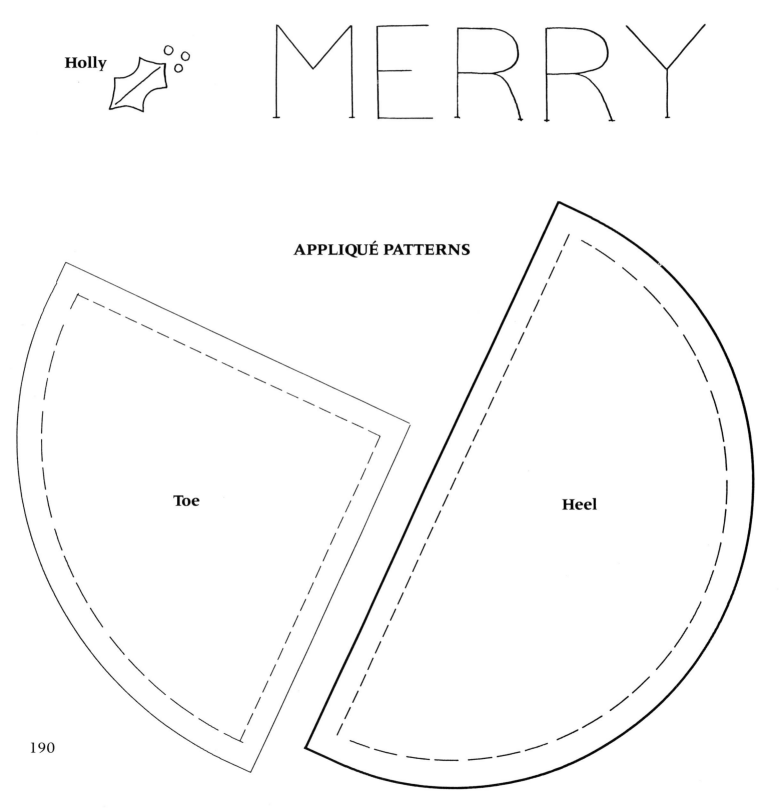

Toe

Heel

190

FULL-SIZE Z-CROSS BLOCK TEMPLATES

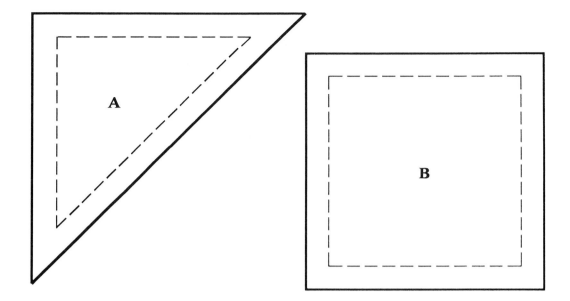

MINI Z-CROSS BLOCK TEMPLATES

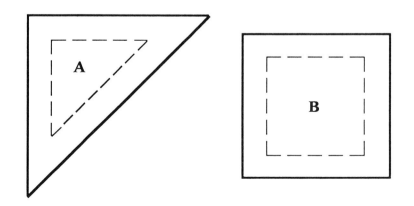

Patchwork Alphabet Quilt

◆◆◆◆◆◆◆◆◆◆◆◆◆◆◆◆◆◆◆◆◆◆◆◆◆◆◆◆◆◆◆◆◆◆◆◆

I was four years old the autumn I entered kindergarten in the Santa Fe Elementary School in Monrovia, California. My first year of school was a very special one, filled with new and exciting ideas and activities. The creative projects were especially thrilling and made me feel that I was accomplishing something really important, whether it was whipping cream into butter or drawing pictures with big, rainbow-colored crayons.

My favorite part of kindergarten was when my teacher, Miss Daley, taught the alphabet. That's when my fascination with the alphabet began, a fascination that has lasted through the years. Now I use the letters not only in reading and writing, but also in my quilting.

I have seen many alphabet quilts, and they have all had full-size letter blocks set in rows and columns that were the center of the quilt. The Patchwork Alphabet Quilt is different: It has 5″ × 5″ mini blocks throughout, and the letters are set in a clockwise direction around a Pinwheel block center. The project uses the bright rainbow colors of kindergarten crayons, which are set against a white background for maximum contrast.

◆◆◆◆◆◆

Mini blocks: **5″ × 5″**
Quilt: **65½″ × 75½″**
Seam allowance: **¼″**

◆◆◆◆◆◆

SUPPLIES

Fabric:

    3 yards white solid
    ¼ yard red solid
    1½ yards red print
    ¼ yard orange solid
    ¼ yard yellow solid
    ¼ yard medium green solid
    ¼ yard bright blue solid
    2¾ yards dark blue solid
    ¼ yard light purple solid
    4½ yards desired color, for backing

Batting: 4 yards

CUTTING GUIDE

For Ducks and Ducklings Block (make 6)*
  A: 12 white
      4 red solid
  B: 4 red solid
  C: 5 white solid
      4 red print

Refer to Ducks and Ducklings Framed Picture (page 41). Use templates for mini Ducks and Ducklings block.

For Red Pinwheel Block (make 20)
  D: 4 white
      4 red print

For Blue Pinwheel Block (make 40)
  D: 4 white
      4 dark blue

For "A" Block
  #7: 1 white
  #8: 1 red solid
  #9: 1 white

#10:   1 red solid
#11:   1 red solid
#12:   2 white (1 reversed)

For "B" Block
#1:   4 white
       5 orange
#2:   2 orange
#3:   2 white
       1 orange
#4:   1 white
       3 orange
#13:   1 white
       1 orange

For "C" Block
#1:   10 white
       10 yellow
#2:   3 white
#4:   1 white
       3 yellow

For "D" Block
#1:   6 white
       6 green
#2:   1 white
#4:   2 white
       4 green

For "E" Block
#1:   4 white
       4 bright blue
#2:   2 white
       1 bright blue
#3:   2 white
#4:   1 white
       1 bright blue
#5:   2 bright blue

For "F" Block
#1:   4 white
       4 dark blue
#2:   2 white
       1 dark blue
#4:   2 white
#5:   1 white
       2 dark blue

For "G" Block
#1:   4 white
       4 purple
#2:   3 white
       3 purple
#4:   3 purple
#15:   1 white

For "H" Block
#1:   4 white
       4 red solid
#2:   1 red solid
#3:   2 white
#4:   2 white
#6:   2 red solid

For "I" Block
#1:   4 white
       4 orange
#4:   2 white
#6:   2 white
       1 orange

For "J" Block
#1:   4 white
       4 yellow
#2:   1 white
       4 yellow
#4:   3 white
       1 yellow
#5:   1 white

For "K" Block
#1:   2 white
       2 green
#4:   1 white
#6:   1 green
#20:   2 white
#21:   1 white
#30:   1 green
#31:   1 green

For "L" Block
#1:   3 white
       3 bright blue
#3:   1 white

#4: 1 white
1 bright blue
#6: 1 bright blue
#16: 1 white

For "M" Block
#6: 2 dark blue
#17: 2 white (1 reversed)
2 dark blue (1 reversed)
#18: 2 white (1 reversed)
2 dark blue (1 reversed)
#22: 1 dark blue

For "N" Block
#6: 2 purple
#23: 2 white
#32: 1 purple

For "O" Block
#1: 8 white
8 red solid
#2: 2 white
#4: 1 white
4 red solid

For "P" Block
#1: 4 white
4 orange
#2: 1 orange
#3: 2 white
2 orange
#4: 1 white
#6: 1 orange
#14: 1 white

For "Q" Block
#1: 8 white
8 yellow
#2: 2 white
#4: 1 white
4 yellow
#40: 1 yellow

For "R" Block
#1: 4 white
4 green
#2: 1 green

#3: 2 white
2 green
#4: 1 white
#6: 1 green
#19: 2 white
2 green

For "S" Block
#1: 4 white
4 bright blue
#2: 2 bright blue
#4: 2 bright blue
#5: 2 white
#6: 1 bright blue

For "T" Block
#1: 4 white
4 dark blue
#2: 4 white
#5: 1 dark blue
#6: 1 dark blue
#14: 2 white

For "U" Block
#1: 4 white
4 purple
#2: 1 white
#4: 1 purple
#5: 2 purple
#16: 1 white

For "V" Block
#10: 1 red solid
#11: 1 red solid
#12: 2 white (1 reversed)
#24: 1 white

For "W" Block
#6: 2 orange
#17: 2 white (1 reversed)
2 orange (1 reversed)
#18: 2 white (1 reversed)
2 orange (1 reversed)
#22: 1 orange

For "X" Block
#25: 2 white

#26: 2 white
#33: 2 yellow
#34: 1 yellow

For "Y" Block
#1: 2 white
    2 green
#2: 2 white
#3: 2 white
    1 green
#27: 1 white
#28: 2 white (1 reversed)
#35: 1 green
#36: 1 green

For "Z" Block
#1: 2 white
    2 bright blue
#29: 2 white
#37: 2 white
#38: 1 bright blue
#39: 2 bright blue

Additional Pieces
E (1½"-wide strip):
    15 white, 5½"
    4 white, 23½"
    2 white, 29½"
F (3½"-wide strip): 2 white, 25½"
G (5½"-wide strip):
    2 white, 35½"
    2 white, 45½"
    2 white, 55½"
    2 white, 75½"
Backing: 69½" × 79½"
Batting: 65½" × 75½"
Binding: 8 yards dark blue solid

DIRECTIONS

Make 26 mini letter blocks, one for each letter of the alphabet, following step-by-step directions beginning on page 199.

Make six mini Ducks and Ducklings blocks; see Ducks and Ducklings Framed Picture: Substitute red solid A's for medium A's, red solid B's for dark B's, and red print C's for light C's.

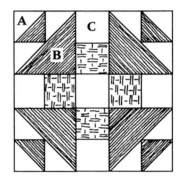

Make 20 red and 40 blue Pinwheel blocks as follows.

Pinwheel Block

Step 1: Sew together a white D and a nonwhite D, to form a square. (Make 4 white/nonwhite squares.)

Step 2: Join the four squares, completing the block.

Assembling the Quilt Center

Stitch together four red Pinwheel blocks and three 5½" E's, to form a row.

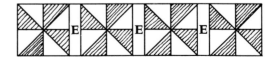

Make four more rows in same manner. Join pieced rows and 23½" E's; see Quilt Center Diagram. Stitch 29½" E's to patchwork sides. Stitch F's to patchwork top and bottom.

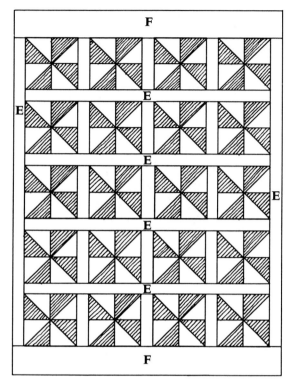

QUILT CENTER DIAGRAM

Borders

Assemble and attach pieced and plain borders to quilt center as follows (see Quilt Diagram).

For alphabet border: For border top, sew together letter blocks horizontally to spell "BCDEF." For right border side, sew together blocks vertically to spell "GHIJKLMN." For border bottom, sew together blocks horizontally to spell "SRQPO." For left side, sew together blocks vertically to spell "AZYXWVUT."
Stitch one Ducks and Ducklings block to bottom of each side strip. Stitch top and bottom strips in place on quilt center; stitch side strips in place.

For inner plain border: Stitch 35½" G's to patchwork top and bottom; stitch 45½" G's to sides.

For Pinwheel border: Sew together blue Pinwheel blocks, to form two 9-block strips and two 11-block strips. Stitch one Ducks and Ducklings block to each end of 11-block strips. Stitch shorter strips to top and bottom of patchwork; stitch longer strips to sides.

For outer plain border: Stitch 55½" G's to patchwork top and bottom; stitch 75½" G's to sides.

Quilting

Transfer scallop motif to both F's, centered between upper and lower strip edges; see "The Quilt Layers" on page 15. Transfer cable motif all around inner plain border. Mark quilting lines on outer plain border; see Quilt Diagram.
Set quilt front, batting, and backing together. Referring to "Quilting" (page 15), baste piece for quilting. Quilt motifs and marked straight lines.

Finishing

Trim backing even with quilt front and batting. Bind quilt edges with dark blue solid fabric; see "Finishing the Quilt" on page 17.

QUILT DIAGRAM

198

Letter Blocks

♦♦♦♦♦♦♦♦♦

"A" BLOCK

Step 1: Stitch #7 and #9 to #8.

Step 2: Sew together #10 and #12.

Step 3: Join pieces from Steps 1 and 2.

Step 4: Sew together #11 and #12R.

Step 5: Join pieces from Steps 3 and 4, completing the block.

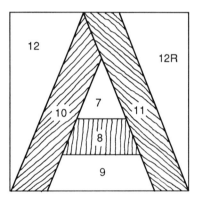

"B" BLOCK

Step 1: Sew together a white #1 and a nonwhite #1, to form a square. (Make 4 white/nonwhite squares.)

Step 2: Stitch two white/nonwhite squares to a nonwhite #4, to form Row 1.

Step 3: Sew together a nonwhite #2 and a white #3, to form a strip. (Make two white/nonwhite strips.)

Step 4: Sew together #13's.

Step 5: Stitch a nonwhite #1 to piece from Step 4.

Step 6: Stitch nonwhite #3 to piece from Step 5.

Step 7: Sew together pieces from Steps 3 and 6, to form right section of combined Rows 2–4.

Step 8: Sew together a white #4 and a nonwhite #4, to form left section of combined Rows 2–4.

Step 9: Join pieces from Steps 7 and 8, to complete Rows 2–4.

Step 10: Repeat Step 2, to form Row 5 (note different orientation of squares).

Step 11: Join Rows 1–5, completing the block.

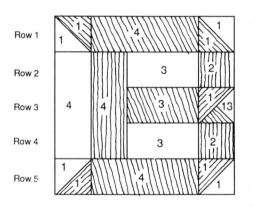

"C" BLOCK

Step 1: Sew together a white #1 and a nonwhite #1, to form a square. (Make 10 white/nonwhite squares.)

Step 2: Stitch two white/nonwhite squares to a nonwhite #4, to form Row 1.

Step 3: Sew together three white/nonwhite squares and a white #2, to form right section of Row 2.

Step 4: Sew together a #2 and a white #4, to form right section of Row 3.

Step 5: Repeat Step 3, to form right section of Row 4 (note different placement of squares).

Step 6: Stitch pieces from Steps 3–5 together, to form right section of combined Rows 2–4.

Step 7: Join nonwhite #4 to piece from Step 6, to complete Rows 2–4.

Step 8: Repeat Step 2, to form Row 5.

Step 9: Join Rows 1–5, completing the block.

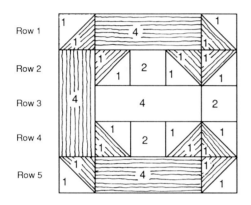

"D" BLOCK

Step 1: Sew together a white #1 and a nonwhite #1, to form a square. (Make 6 white/nonwhite squares.)

Step 2: Stitch two white/nonwhite squares to a white #4, to form Row 1.

Step 3: Stitch two white/nonwhite squares to a white #2, to form center of Row 4.

Step 4: Stitch a nonwhite #4 and piece from Step 3 to a white #4, to form center of combined Rows 2–4.

Step 5: Join two nonwhite #4's to piece from Step 4, to complete Rows 2–4.

Step 6: Stitch two white/nonwhite squares to a nonwhite #4, to form Row 5.

Step 7: Join Rows 1–5, completing the block.

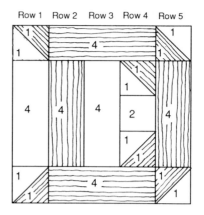

"E" BLOCK

Step 1: Sew together a white #1 and a nonwhite #1, to form a square. (Make 4 white/nonwhite squares.)

Step 2: Sew together a white/nonwhite square and a nonwhite #5, to form Row 1.

Step 3: Sew together a white/nonwhite square and a #3, to form right section of Row 2.

Step 4: Sew together two white #2's and a nonwhite #2, to form right section of Row 3.

Step 5: Repeat Step 3, to form right section of Row 4 (note different orientation of square).

Step 6: Stitch pieces from Steps 3–5 together, to form right section of combined Rows 2–4.

Step 7: Sew together white #4 and nonwhite #4, to form left section of combined Rows 2–4.

Step 8: Join pieces from Steps 6 and 7, to complete Rows 2–4.

Step 9: Repeat Step 2, to form Row 5 (note different orientation of square).

Step 10: Join Rows 1–5, completing the block.

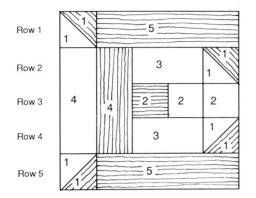

"F" BLOCK

Step 1: Sew together a white #1 and a nonwhite #1, to form a square. (Make 4 white/nonwhite squares.)

Step 2: Stitch two white/nonwhite squares to a #4, to form Row 1.

Step 3: Sew together a white/nonwhite square, two white #2's, and a nonwhite #2, to form bottom of Row 3.

Step 4: Sew together a white/nonwhite square and a #4, to form bottom of Row 5.

Step 5: Sew together a white #5, a nonwhite #5, and pieces from Steps 3 and 4, to form bottom of combined Rows 2–5.

Step 6: Join a nonwhite #5 to piece from Step 5, to complete Rows 2–5.

Step 7: Join Row 1 to combined Rows 2–5, completing the block.

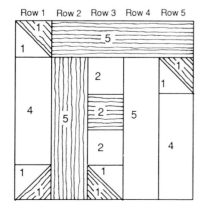

"G" BLOCK

Step 1: Sew together a white #1 and a nonwhite #1, to form a square. (Make 4 white/nonwhite squares.)

Step 2: Stitch two white/nonwhite squares to a #4, to form Row 1.

Step 3: Sew together two white #2's.

Step 4: Sew together two nonwhite #2's.

Step 5: Sew together a white #2 and a nonwhite #2.

Step 6: Stitch pieces from Steps 3–5 together, to form right section of combined Rows 2–4.

Step 7: Sew together a #4 and white #15, to form left section of combined Rows 2–4.

Step 8: Join pieces from Steps 6 and 7, to complete Rows 2–4.

Step 9: Repeat Step 2, to form Row 5.

Step 10: Join Rows 1–5, completing the block.

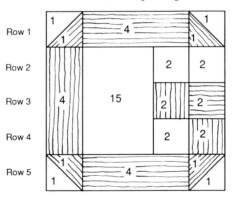

"H" BLOCK

Step 1: Sew together a white #1 and a nonwhite #1, to form a square. (Make 4 white/nonwhite squares.)

Step 2: Stitch two white/nonwhite squares to a #4, to form Row 1.

Step 3: Stitch #3's to #2, to form Row 3.

Step 4: Repeat Step 2, to form Row 5.

Step 5: Join Rows 1–5, completing the block.

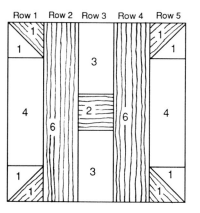

"I" BLOCK

Step 1: Sew together a white #1 and a nonwhite #1, to form a square. (Make 4 white/nonwhite squares.)

Step 2: Stitch two white/nonwhite squares to a #4, to form Row 2.

Step 3: Repeat Step 2, to form Row 4.

Step 4: Join Rows 1–5, completing the block.

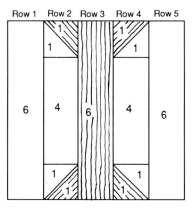

"J" BLOCK

Step 1: Sew together a white #1 and a nonwhite #1, to form a square. (Make 4 white/nonwhite squares.)

Step 2: Stitch a white/nonwhite square and a white #4 to a nonwhite #2, to form Row 1.

Step 3: Stitch #5 and a nonwhite #2 together, to form Row 2.

Step 4: Stitch a white/nonwhite square and a nonwhite #2 to a white #4, to form Row 3.

Step 5: Stitch a white/nonwhite square and a nonwhite #2 to a nonwhite #4, to form Row 4.

Step 6: Stitch a white/nonwhite square and a white #2 to a white #4, to form Row 5.

Step 7: Join Rows 1–5, completing the block.

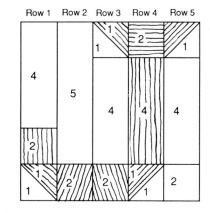

"K" BLOCK

Step 1: Sew together a white #1 and a nonwhite #1, to form a square. (Make 2 white/nonwhite squares.)

Step 2: Stitch two white/nonwhite squares to #4, to form Row 1.

Step 3: Sew together a #20 and #30.

Step 4: Stitch a #20 and #21 to #31.

Step 5: Join pieces from Steps 3 and 4, to complete Row 3.

Step 6: Join Rows 1–3, completing the block.

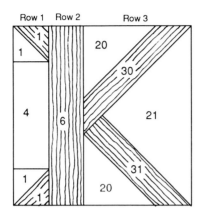

"L" BLOCK

Step 1: Sew together a white #1 and a nonwhite #1, to form a square. (Make 3 white/nonwhite squares.)

Step 2: Stitch two white/nonwhite squares to white #4, to form Row 1.

Step 3: Sew together a white/nonwhite square and #3.

Step 4: Join nonwhite #4 and #16 to piece from Step 3, to complete Row 3.

Step 5: Join Rows 1–3, completing the block.

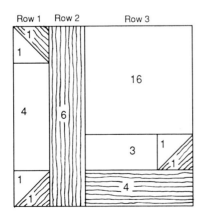

"M" BLOCK

Step 1: Sew together #17's, to form a rectangle.

Step 2: Sew together #17R's.

Step 3: Sew together pieces from Steps 1 and 2.

Step 4: Sew together #18's.

Step 5: Sew together #18R's.

Step 6: Stitch pieces from Steps 4 and 5 to #22.

Step 7: Join pieces from Steps 3 and 6, to complete Row 2.

Step 8: Join Rows 1–3, completing the block.

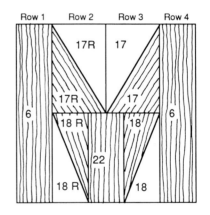

"N" BLOCK

Step 1: Stitch #23's to #32, to form Row 2.

Step 2: Join Rows 1–3, completing the block.

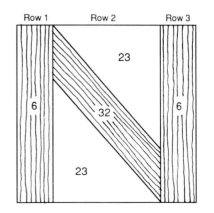

"O" BLOCK

Step 1: Sew together a white #1 and a nonwhite #1, to form a square. (Make 8 white/nonwhite squares.)

Step 2: Stitch two white/nonwhite squares to a nonwhite #4, to form Row 1.

Step 3: Stitch two white/nonwhite squares to a #2, to form a strip. (Make 2 white/nonwhite strips.)

Step 4: Stitch white #4 and pieces from Step 3 together, to form center of combined Rows 2–4.

Step 5: Join two nonwhite #4's to piece from Step 4, to complete Rows 2–4.

Step 6: Repeat Step 2, to form Row 5.

Step 7: Join Rows 1–5, completing the block.

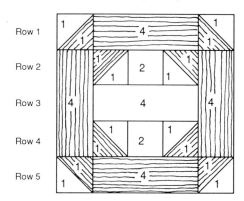

"P" BLOCK

Step 1: Sew together a white #1 and a nonwhite #1, to form a square. (Make 4 white/nonwhite squares.)

Step 2: Stitch two white/nonwhite squares to #4, to form Row 1.

Step 3: Sew together a white #3, two nonwhite #3's, and #14, to form Row 3.

Step 4: Sew together two white/nonwhite squares, #2, and a white #3, to form Row 4.

Step 5: Join Rows 1–4, completing the block.

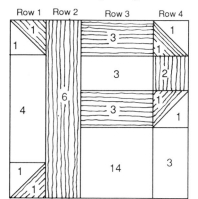

"Q" BLOCK

Step 1: Follow step-by-step directions for "O" block.

Step 2: Appliqué #40 (tail) on block as shown; see "Appliqué" on page 13.

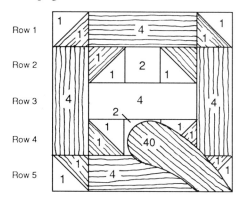

"R" BLOCK

Step 1: Sew together a white #1 and a nonwhite #1, to form a square. (Make 4 white/nonwhite squares.)

Step 2: Stitch two white/nonwhite squares to #4, to form Row 1.

Step 3: Sew together a white #19 and a nonwhite #19, to form a rectangle. (Make 2 white/nonwhite rectangles.)

Step 4: Sew together a white/nonwhite rectangle and a white #3, to form bottom of Row 3.

Step 5: Join a white #3, two nonwhite #3's, and piece from Step 4, to complete Row 3.

Step 6: Sew together two white/nonwhite squares, a white/nonwhite rectangle, and #2, to form Row 4.

Step 7: Join Rows 1–4, completing the block.

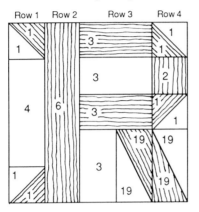

"S" BLOCK

Step 1: Sew together a white #1 and a nonwhite #1, to form a square. (Make 4 white/nonwhite squares.)

Step 2: Stitch two white/nonwhite squares to a #4, to form Row 1.

Step 3: Sew together a #2 and a #5, to form Row 2.

Step 4: Repeat Step 3, to form Row 4.

Step 5: Repeat Step 2, to form Row 5.

Step 6: Join Rows 1–5, completing the block.

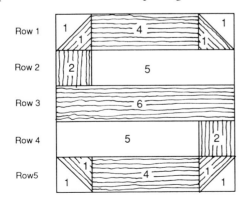

"T" BLOCK

Step 1: Sew together a white #1 and a nonwhite #1, to form a square. (Make 4 white/nonwhite squares.)

Step 2: Sew together a white/nonwhite square and a #2, to form a rectangle. (Make 2 rectangles.)

Step 3: Stitch both rectangles from Step 2 to a #14, to form left section of combined Rows 2–4.

Step 4: Repeat Steps 2 and 3, to form right section of combined Rows 2–4 (note different orientation of squares).

Step 5: Join pieces from Steps 3 and 4 to #5, to complete Rows 2–4.

Step 6: Join Rows 1–4, completing the block.

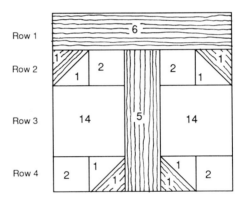

"U" BLOCK

Step 1: Sew together a white #1 and a nonwhite #1, to form a square. (Make 4 white/nonwhite squares.)

Step 2: Stitch two white/nonwhite squares to #2, to form center of Row 2.

Step 3: Sew together #16 and piece from Step 2, to form center of combined Rows 1 and 2.

Step 4: Join #5's to piece from Step 3, to complete Rows 1 and 2.

205

Step 5: Stitch two white/nonwhite squares to #4, to form Row 3.

Step 6: Join Rows 1–3, completing the block.

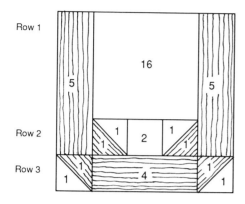

"V" BLOCK

Step 1: Sew together #11 and #12R.

Step 2: Stitch #12 and #24 to #10.

Step 3: Join pieces from Steps 1 and 2, completing the block.

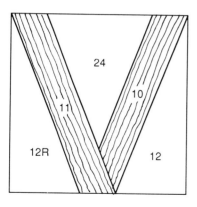

"W" BLOCK

Step 1: Follow step-by-step directions for "M" block.

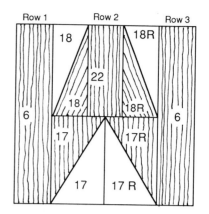

"X" BLOCK

Step 1: Stitch a #25 and a #26 to a #33, to form a triangle. (Make 2 white/nonwhite triangles.)

Step 2: Join pieces from Step 1 to #34, completing the block.

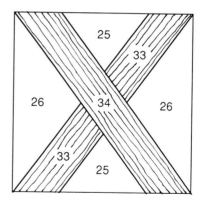

"Y" BLOCK

Step 1: Sew together #28 and #35.

Step 2: Stitch #27 and #28R to #36.

Step 3: Join pieces from Steps 1 and 2, to form Row 1.

Step 4: Sew together a white #1 and a nonwhite #1, to form a square. (Make 2 white/nonwhite squares.)

Step 5: Sew together a white/nonwhite square, a #2, and a white #3, to form left section of combined Rows 2 and 3.

Step 6: Repeat Step 5, to form right section of combined Rows 2 and 3 (note different orientation of white/nonwhite square).

Step 7: Join pieces from Steps 5 and 6 to nonwhite #3, to complete Rows 2 and 3.

Step 8: Join Rows 1–3, completing the block.

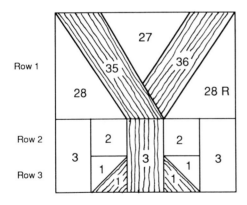

"Z" BLOCK

Step 1: Sew together a white #1 and a nonwhite #1, to form a square. (Make 2 white/nonwhite squares.)

Step 2: Sew together a white/nonwhite square and a #37.

Step 3: Sew together a #29 and piece from Step 2, to form a triangle.

Step 4: Repeat Steps 2 and 3, to form another triangle.

Step 5: Stitch pieces from Steps 3 and 4 to #38.

Step 6: Join #39's to piece from Step 5, completing the block.

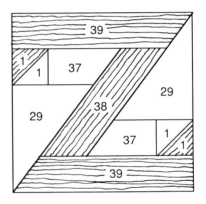

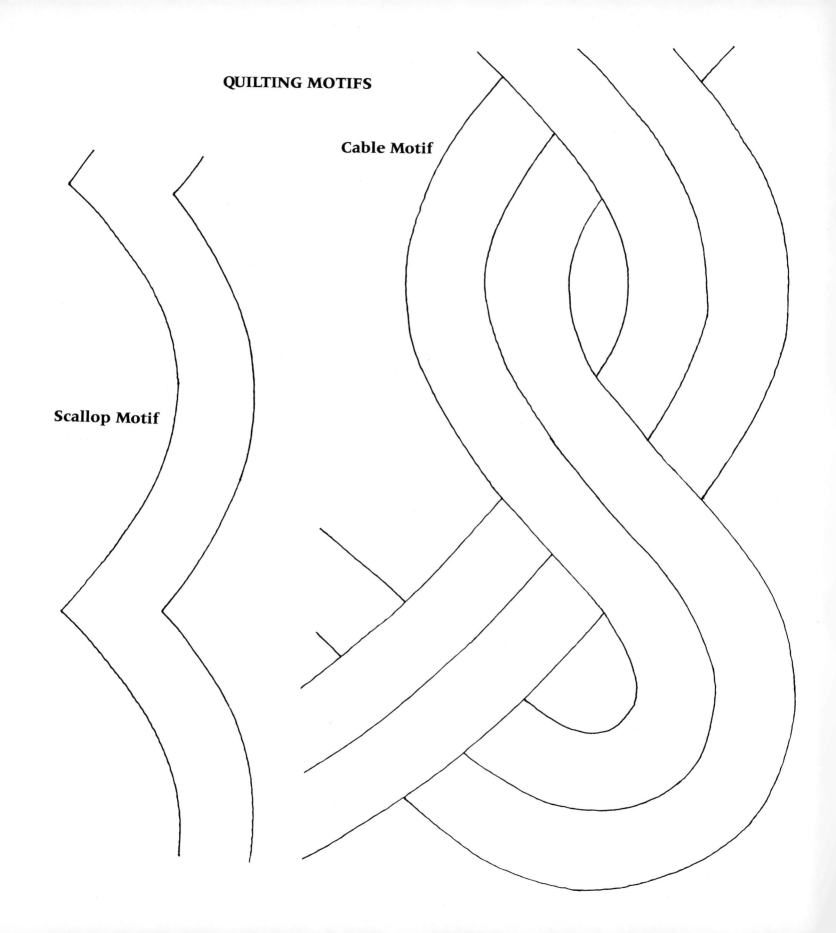

QUILTING MOTIFS

Cable Motif

Scallop Motif

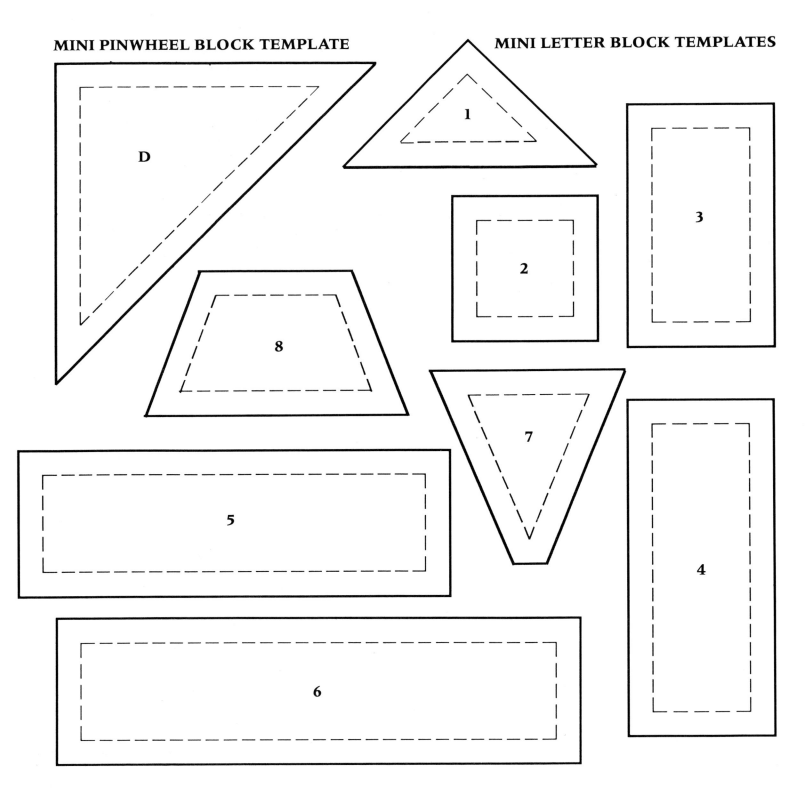

MINI PINWHEEL BLOCK TEMPLATE

MINI LETTER BLOCK TEMPLATES

D

1

2

3

8

7

5

4

6

209

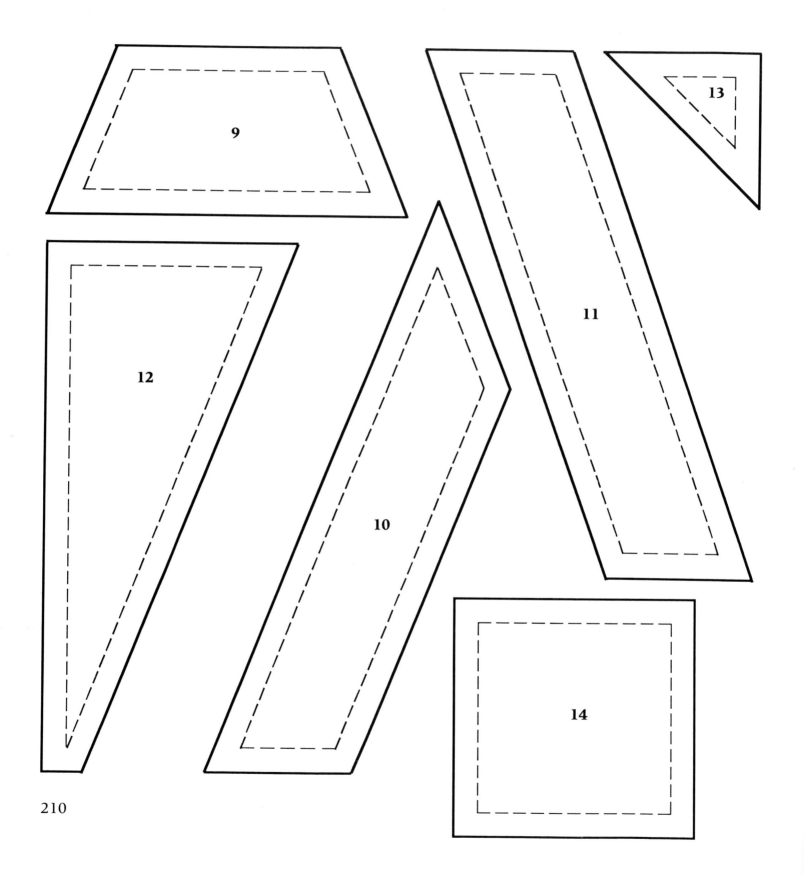

9

13

11

12

10

14

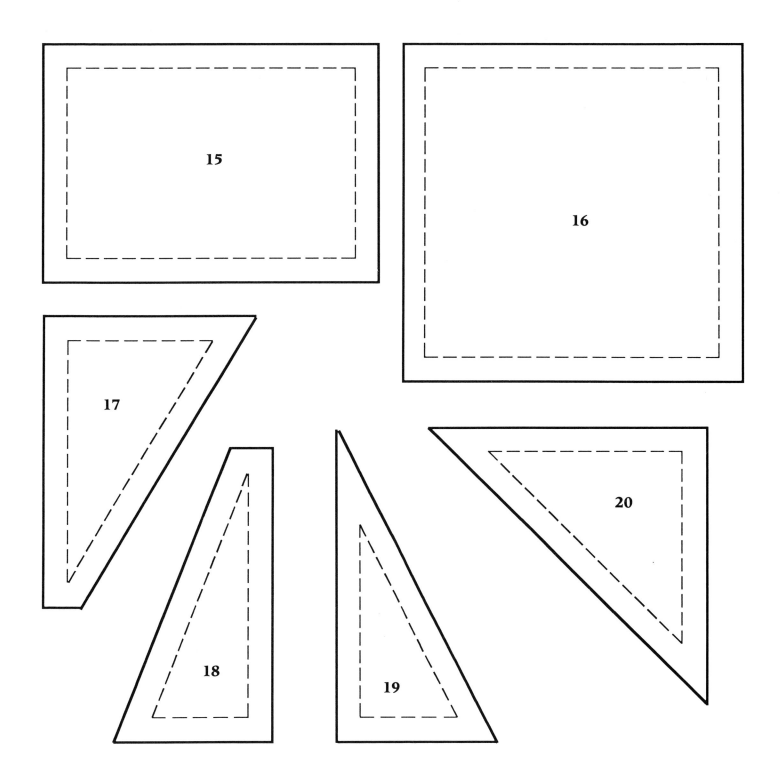

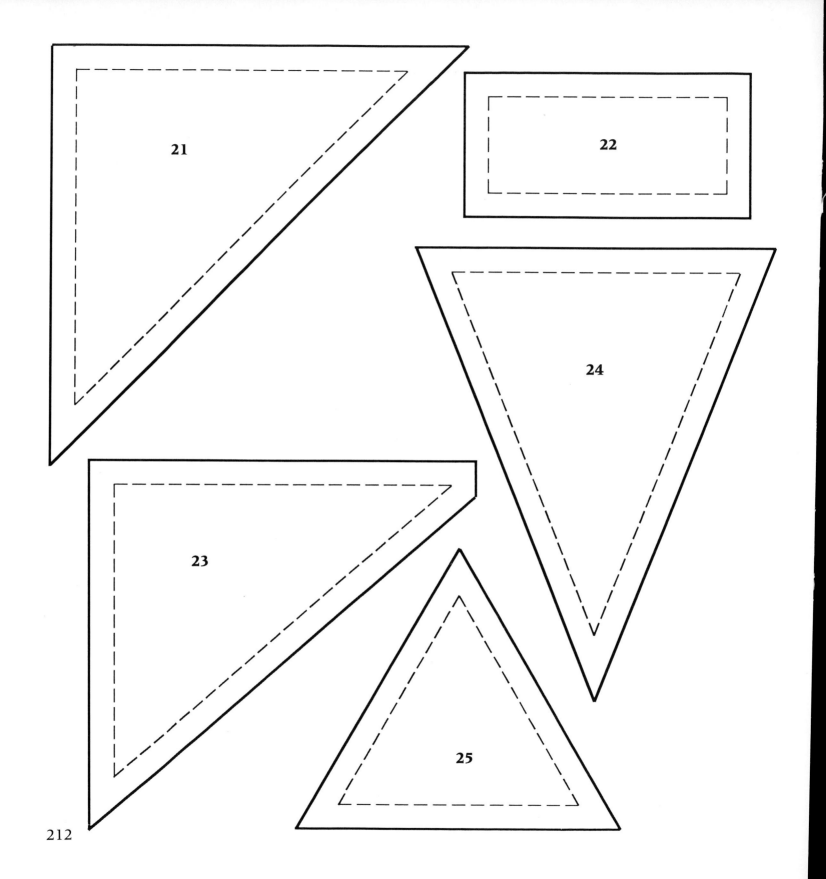

21

22

23

24

25

212

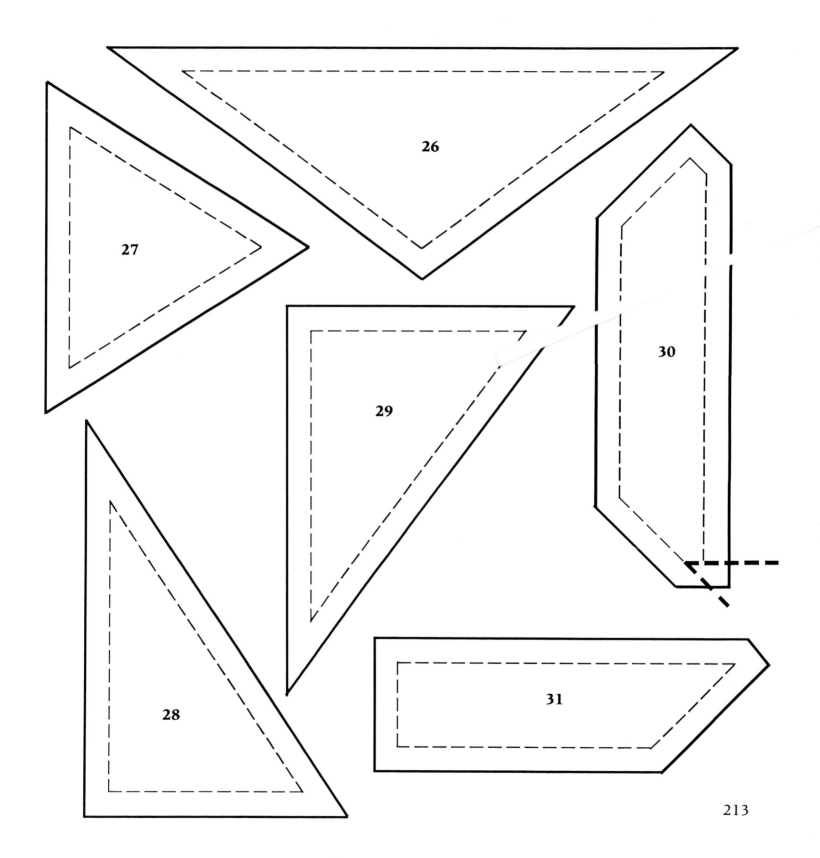

26

27

29

30

28

31

213

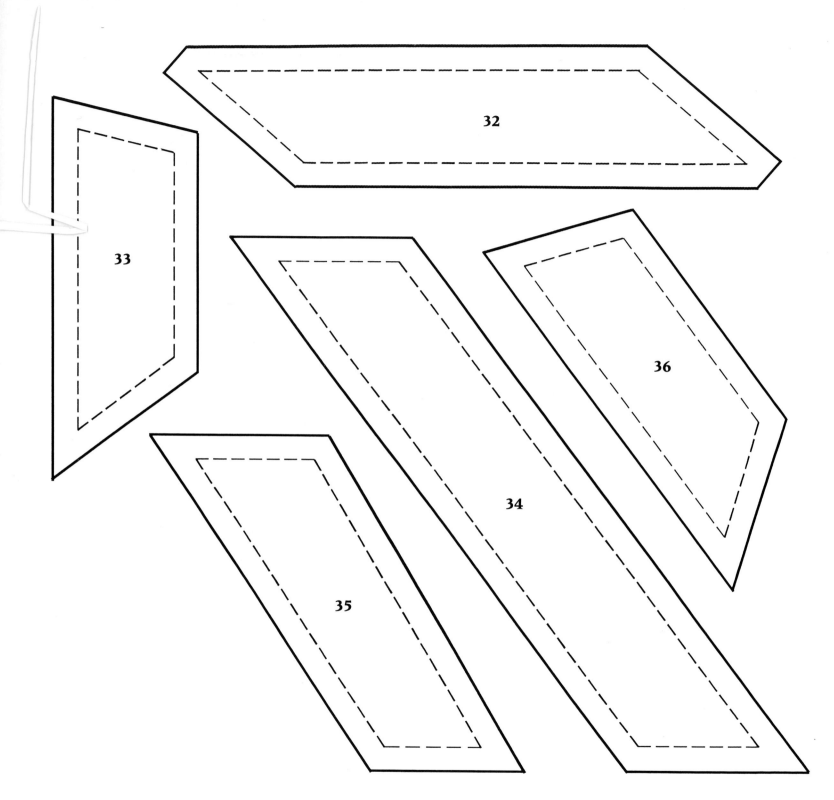

32

33

34

35

36

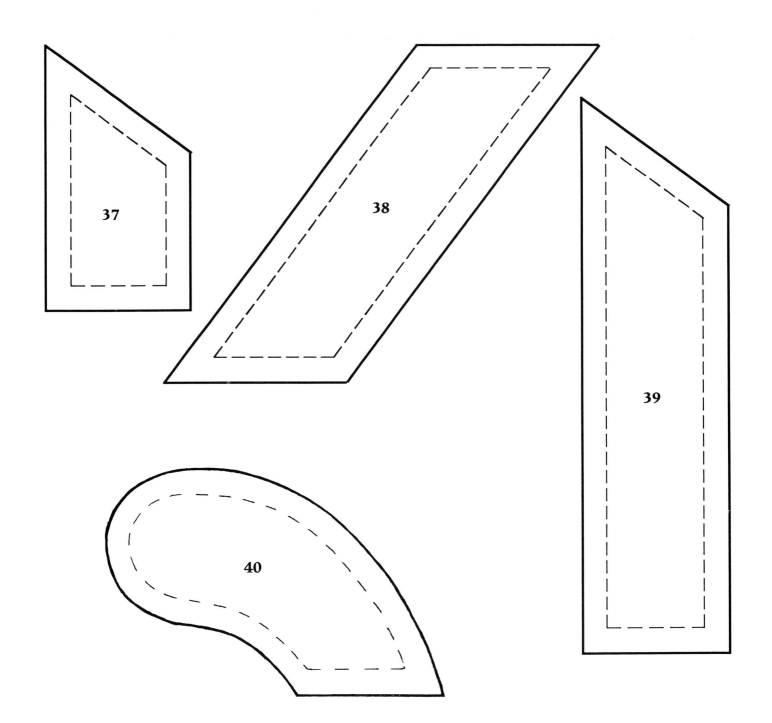

37

38

39

40

INDEX

All of us at Meredith® Press welcome your comments and suggestions so that we may continue providing you with the best crafts products possible. Please address your correspondence to Customer Service Department, Meredith® Press, 150 East 52nd Street, New York, NY 10022, or call 1-800-678-2665.